"Coach Madison changed the trajectory of ———— a better husband, coach, ———————————— n- torship. For thirty years ———————————— t crossroads, and the wis———————————— - tained and guided me th———————————— these pages you'll find th———————— with me and so many others t— —gnout baseball. I'd encourage you to invest the time in the book and enjoy the growth and clarity that comes from spending time alongside Coach."

— *Andy Green*
Senior Vice-President, New York Mets

"Keith Madison's *Coaching with Purpose* is a profound guide on leading and developing young people through baseball. As one of the highest-character individuals I have had the pleasure to know, Keith embodies integrity, wisdom, and respect, qualities that shine through in this book. With Hall of Fame coaching credentials and a lifetime dedicated to serving others, Keith's love for baseball and his passion for mentoring others are evident in every chapter. This book will inspire coaches to connect with their players in a more impactful and meaningful way, while also providing invaluable insights on creating a vision, building a culture of character, and fostering resilience. A must-read for anyone looking to lead with purpose, both on and off the field."

— *Craig Keilitz*
Executive Director of the American Baseball Coaches Association

"This book is perfect for coaches at any stage in their career. Keith Madison is a Hall of Fame coach, in part, because Coach Madison is just as good at coaching baseball as he is coaching the person."

—*NICK MINGIONE*
Head Baseball Coach, University of Kentucky

"I've been fortunate to be around a lot of great mentors and coaches in my journey through baseball. Coach Madison's impact on coaches, players, and families has stood out as much as any of them. The game of baseball (or any sport) is a platform God has given us to impact people for His glory. The sooner we can understand and maximize that, the sooner we realize our greater purpose in this industry. Coach Madison's experience and example has touched an incredible amount of lives across the world. I'm excited that, through this book, coaches can get a glimpse of how the joy and peace of Christ being the center of our job can drive us each day to a mission far greater than the game played on the field."

—*CASEY DYKES*
Hitting Coach, New York Yankees

"Actually couldn't put it down... what an insightful description of the importance of what we do. The coaching profession is a life work about connecting with people. Keith Madison outlines this and how we can impact players through this plan. I will definitely refer to it again and again. We are all under construction in this business, Keith creates a thoughtful foundation for us to build on!"

—*PAT MURPHY*
Manager, Milwaukee Brewers

"I have evaluated and viewed Coach Keith Madison from several different lenses. Being a SEC head coach a generation before me, he provided an amazing example of how to run a program and more importantly to love your players and lead a life that is bigger than ball. I have so appreciated the friendship, help along the way and even speaking at our banquet. *Coaching with Purpose* is a blueprint and legacy piece for one of the best difference makers SEC baseball has ever known."

—*BUTCH THOMPSON*
Head Baseball Coach, Auburn University

"As a Division I Coach for 30 years, it's easy to read this book and wish I would of read it before I put on my first coaching hat. But fortunately, it's still not too late. Coach Madison has been pouring into hundreds and even thousands of coaches on a daily basis for many years. And I'm blessed to be one of them receiving daily text messages as well as offering his time to speak at a team chapel from time to time. But he changed my life when he encouraged me to attend a baseball mission trip to the Dominican Republic with SCORE International, inspiring me to take my first of three different teams ('15, '19, '23) to the DR to share the Love of Jesus with others, what Coach Madison has been doing for a long time. I challenge you to read this book and let a flame get lit in you so you can truly make the impact on others that God has called you to do."

—*Dan McDonnell*
Head Baseball Coach, University of Louisville

"I had the opportunity to watch Keith Madison go from one of my Graduate Assistants to battling for wins in the best league in America. While he was at Mississippi State, I quickly moved him into the role of Pitching Coach. Then at Kentucky, as the head coach, Keith always had his teams prepared and competitive, but you could also see how much he cared for his players. You don't get the number of wins he has without pouring into the person as well. After Keith and I both retired, I traveled to the Dominican Republic with him at least ten times to help conduct free baseball clinics for thousands of young Dominican baseball players. It was rewarding to serve alongside my former Graduate Assistant and friend, Keith Madison. This book is packed with helpful ways to coach, guide, and lead each player on your team. I recommend it without hesitation."

—*RON POLK*
Former Head Baseball Coach at Georgia Southern,
Georgia, and Mississippi State

"After reading Coach Madison's new book, *Coaching with Purpose*, I felt like I had literally taken a trip around the bases ... and scored.

Keith shares his life experiences in engaging narrative and challenges us to dig in to our own coaching purpose. He covers the wonderful game of baseball as well as the people he has coached and learned from with grace and humility.

Book it! Pun intended."

—*CLINT HURDLE*
Former MLB Outfielder and Manager

COACHING WITH PURPOSE

The Game Plan That Helps Coaches Build
Winners on and off the Field

KEITH MADISON

XULON ELITE

Xulon Press Elite
555 Winderley Pl, Suite 225
Maitland, FL 32751
407.339.4217
www.xulonpress.com

© 2024 by Keith Madison

All rights reserved solely by the author. The author guarantees all contents are original and do not infringe upon the legal rights of any other person or work. No part of this book may be reproduced in any form without the permission of the author.

Due to the changing nature of the Internet, if there are any web addresses, links, or URLs included in this manuscript, these may have been altered and may no longer be accessible. The views and opinions shared in this book belong solely to the author and do not necessarily reflect those of the publisher. The publisher therefore disclaims responsibility for the views or opinions expressed within the work.

All Scripture quotations, unless otherwise indicated, are taken from the Holy Bible, New International Version®, NIV®. Copyright ©1973, 1978, 1984, 2011 by Biblica, Inc.™ Used by permission of Zondervan. All rights reserved worldwide. www.zondervan.com The "NIV" and "New International Version" are trademarks registered in the United States Patent and Trademark Office by Biblica, Inc.™

Cover and graphics designed by T. Madison
Cover photo by G Visuals on Unsplash

Paperback ISBN-13: 979-8-86850-676-5
Hard Cover ISBN-13: 979-8-86850-677-2
Ebook ISBN-13: 979-8-86850-678-9

To my wife, Sharon.

You are a hall of fame wife, my best friend, and an incredible teammate. Thanks for believing in me.

Table of Contents

1. We Coach Players, Not a Game. 1

Part 1: FIRST BASE – *Craft a Vision* 9
  2. Let's Win Something Today!. 11
  3. Know Where You're Heading: Building a
     Personal Vision 17
  4. Know Your Identity. 29
  5. Take Your Team: Developing a Vision for
     Your Program. 39

Part 2: SECOND BASE – *Build Alignment*. 49
  6. Turning Vision into Reality. 51
  7. Communication. 63
  8. Winning Culture 77

Part 3: THIRD BASE – *Champion Execution*. 93
  9. Decision Making 95
  10. Bouncing Back. 115
  11. Character Development. 131

Part 4: HOME PLATE – *Make it Home* 143
  12. Carrying the Weight 145
  13. Curve Balls 153

14. Heading for Home..........................161

Acknowledgments..............................177
Notes..183
About the Author 193

- 1 -

We Coach Players, Not a Game

*What you are is God's gift to you,
what you become is your gift to God.*
—*Hans Urs von Balthasar*

THE ANNOUNCERS RAMBLED on in the background as we relaxed in the comfortable leather sectional facing the TV. We'd spent the day out on the river where I'd caught four trout—not bad for my first-time fly fishing. I was having a great time visiting my former player, Jeff, who now lived 9,000 feet above sea level in the beautiful Rocky Mountains. One of the long-lasting blessings of coaching has been the relationships with the young men I've coached. After spending a few days at his mountain cabin, I could see why he'd made Colorado his home.

"Keith, why do I coach? I don't need this," he said as he clicked the channel so we could check the scores on another game.

Jeff, who was now coaching baseball, began to tell me about a call he'd recently received from a parent. After an early morning at the office and a long evening at the ballfield, his phone rang. On the other end of the line, the father of one of his high school players said, "My son wants to play college baseball. In our family *we* play to win. I have hired a private hitting coach and pitching coach to help him. I believe my son should be in the lineup, otherwise how will he earn a spot on a college roster?"

Clearly, the father was frustrated. His son, a junior, was hitting .130 and hadn't performed well enough to secure his position in the lineup. A freshman had taken his position and been playing well. It hadn't been Jeff's first interaction with this parent.

A successful businessman in a region known more for skiing than baseball, Jeff's love of the game led him to keep the passion alive. He wanted to make a difference in the lives of young men the way his baseball coaches had impacted him. And he wanted to contribute to his community. It kept him motivated to face the next challenge. Although practically all the other parents were supportive this year, sometimes it only takes one more challenge to start questioning, "Why do I coach?" I had an answer for him.

During my 28 years of coaching there were challenges, to be sure. When I arrived at the University of Kentucky (UK) the facilities were not up to the standards of most Division 1 programs. We were the only team in the Southeastern Conference (SEC) without a full allotment of scholarships. And at the time I was hired, my "head coach" position was just part-time. This meant that I had no benefits, my salary was less than half of my SEC contemporaries, and I only had $2,000 to pay for one assistant coach.

These were major roadblocks for someone with dreams of becoming a successful coach at the NCAA Division I level. Some folks told me it was impossible. But in my first year at UK, the team turned things around and tallied up the most wins in program history. In my third year, we broke the school record again and finished second in the powerful Eastern Division of the SEC and runner-up in the SEC Tournament, defeating a couple of perennial powers. It was a difficult road, but not impossible.

Today's Challenges

The challenges and pressures facing today's coaches are real.

Depending on the level you coach, you could be facing a lack of funding, a shallow pool of talent, unrealistic expectations from parents, pressure from your athletic director, Name Image Likeness (NIL) obstacles, or uncertainties with the NCAA Transfer Portal.

You may be trying to balance coaching and your day job, not to mention home life and your own family. There may be disciplinary issues within your team or philosophical differences within your staff. You may have zealous parents, or the opposite—kids with no support, no gear, and maybe not even enough food. Any one of these challenges could prevent you from becoming the coach you want to be.

If we're not careful, the challenges can rob us of the joy and impact of coaching—an incredibly rewarding profession. You won't likely become as wealthy as Elon Musk or Aaron Judge, but you will become rich in so many other ways. I can attest to that.

A couple of years after retiring from UK, I was asked to speak at an American Baseball Coaches Association (ABCA) clinic. The topic: "If I Could Do It All Over Again." It's not easy to be transparent in front of thousands of coaches. But being transparent is being truthful. It's a wonderful way to earn trust. It also gave me the opportunity to reflect on my own journey as a coach—a journey that included leaning on coaches I respected and trusted to give me guidance from the time I was just starting out to the end of my coaching career. We all need that. We are all a work in progress.

That presentation at the ABCA clinic began a new desire, a calling, to help coaches to be effective, successful, and transformational. After that day, I received numerous phone calls from coaches who wanted to discuss their careers or their professional and personal situations as a leader of young men. It was evident that God was telling me that I was still a coach but in this new season I'd be coaching coaches instead of players.

Champion Coaches Build Champion People

Coaches are leaders, and there is a desperate need for leaders in our society today. Your role as a coach can make a positive impact on a multitude of players. Those players can then impact a family, a community, and even a state and a nation for generations to come.

Successful leaders know how to connect and influence those who are looking to them for guidance. This book is about equipping you to not only be a championship level *coach*, but to build championship level *people*.

> AT THE END OF THE DAY, WE COACH PLAYERS, NOT A GAME.

When you're a player, you are responsible for a job... throw strikes, produce hits, and make plays. When you become a leader (Coach), you are responsible for the *people* who do the job. It's not about being in charge; it's about taking care of the players in our charge.

At the end of the day, we coach players, not a game.

Influence & Impact

I can't deny it was incredibly rewarding to spend 25 years coaching the Kentucky Wildcats. I inherited a team that had broken the school record for losses the previous year and watched them turn it around to set the school record for wins in my first year. It was gratifying to go on to earn 737 wins in my career at UK, not to mention watching 17 players go on to Major League Baseball, including Joe Blanton, Jim Leyritz, Terry Shumpert, and 2006 Cy Young Award winner Brandon Webb. But there's something even better.

When a player comes back years later and says, "Coach, because of your influence, I'm a better husband and father than I would have been had I not played for you," it is powerful. It doesn't take a well-known coaching position or an award-winning record to accomplish that. Records will be broken. New names will make the news. Wherever you coach—from the local little league to the majors—impact is what lasts.

> RECORDS WILL BE BROKEN. NEW NAMES WILL MAKE THE NEWS. WHEREVER YOU COACH—FROM THE LOCAL LITTLE LEAGUE TO THE MAJORS—IMPACT IS WHAT LASTS.

There are a million books, podcasts, and YouTube videos for coaching tips. Most of them are going to tell you about the latest gear, techniques, or drills. You can go to an ABCA clinic for practice tips or brushing up on your analytics. This book is different. I will be sharing thoughts on leading players and the coaching staff for success on and off the field.

My heart's desire is that this book will encourage you to grow as a coach and a leader of young athletes, that it will help you become the coach that you would have enjoyed playing for. After two years coaching high school baseball, 26 years at the college level, and 20 years of mentoring coaches one-on-one, I've gained a few insights that I believe can help. You don't have to navigate the long and winding road of coaching alone.

Being a successful, impactful coach begins by knowing who you are and where you would like to take your career and your program. That's what we'll talk about in Part 1: Craft a Vision.

In Part 2: Build Alignment, we'll talk about getting your players and staff (even if they're volunteers) on board. Then, in Part 3: Champion Execution, we'll focus on how to navigate challenges along the way. Finally, we'll talk about persevering for the long-haul in Part 4: Home Plate. After all, our goal is to make it home.

You, my friend, have an opportunity. God gave us this gift of baseball. We can use our skills and influence to build a brighter future, and we get to do it through our passion for the game.

Let us not become weary in doing good, for at the proper time we will reap a harvest if we do not give up.
—Galatians 6:9

PART 1:
FIRST BASE

Craft a Vision

- 2 -

Let's Win Something Today!

*You see, you spend a good piece of your life
gripping a baseball, and in the end it turns out
that it was the other way around all the time.
—Jim Bouton*

I'VE ALWAYS LOVED the game of baseball. For me, it all started on an ordinary summer day. My childhood home was on a gravel road about a mile from the nearest paved highway. State Route 259 winds through rural Edmonson County, Kentucky, dodging hills, streams, and "hollers." I was four years old, possibly five. I can't remember the exact year, but from that day on, baseball was part of my life.

Our closest neighbors, the Brownings, lived several hundred yards from our house. Their house, similar to ours, was very small and had no indoor plumbing. We did have electricity and I'm sure the Brownings did as well.

I strolled down the road to see what the Browning boys were doing. They were older than my brother and me, and were always up to something, which is why I noticed the quiet on this particular day. No one was running through the squeaky front door. There was no scratch of the cross saw coming from across the road where the boys were usually cutting firewood. There were no shouts as they tossed logs onto the woodpile or finished their other chores in the front yard.

That's when I heard it; a popping noise echoed from the back of the house. A moment later, I heard it again. I walked around the corner and made myself at home in their backyard.

Two of the brothers stood across from each other, throwing a baseball back and forth. Then, the older of the two squatted in the catcher's stance and began catching and throwing the ball back without ever getting out of his squat. The younger brother, Anthony, was about ten or eleven years old. He was standing with a glove on his left hand, and in a smooth athletic motion, he rocked back with his left leg and then pivoted his right foot before turning his body and releasing the baseball. Pop. It sunk into the catcher's mitt.

As crazy as it sounds, I had never seen anything like that before. We had no television, so I had never seen a baseball game. In those days, any idea of playing consisted of making roads in the dirt near our house and driving my miniature cars around the highways that I had created. This sound, this athletic movement, and the speed of the ball hurling toward the catcher fascinated me. I wanted to try this!

When my dad came home from work that evening, my older brother and I told him that we needed a baseball and gloves so that we could play catch like the Browning boys next door. We were very poor at that time, but we didn't know it. Everyone in our small rural community was just about the same. As poor as we were, my father managed to bring home two gloves and a baseball. I was hooked.

Each day, as soon as my brother, Tommy, came home from school, I would toss him his glove. We threw that ball back and forth until mom called us in for supper. This was a ritual until my brother graduated and left home. It served me well.

Fifteen years after watching the Browning boys play catch, I was 19 years old and already playing Triple A for the Montreal Expos in Winnipeg. I eventually moved on to spend three seasons in the Cincinnati Reds organization. I was living my dream.

In October of 1974, I received a letter that no professional baseball player wants to receive. I was informed that the Cincinnati Reds no longer needed my services. I was released. I was disappointed, of course, but not devastated. I'd already been through the ringer three years before when the Montreal Expos released me at the end of spring training. This time I accepted the news; it was time to start a life "after baseball."

Little did I know what a firm grip baseball had on me! After a year away from the game, I found myself drawn to it once more, this time taking a role as a high school coach.

It only took a few years of coaching to help me realize that even though I loved playing the game, it was even more rewarding to teach other players and help them pursue their dreams. As a player, I couldn't wait to put on the uniform. As a coach, I was the same way. That uniform meant, "Let's win something today!"

As we transition to coaching, loving the game isn't enough. Leading players through the ups and downs of competition, injuries, personal tragedies, slumps, and all types of highs and lows makes coaches see the game in a different way. The transition from playing to coaching isn't seamless, but it can be transformational.

The Stakes Are High

Coaching is one of the most difficult careers to pursue. Sure, outsiders may think you're just playing a game, but you and I both know the stakes are much higher.

> COACHING IS ONE OF THE MOST DIFFICULT CAREERS TO PURSUE. SURE, OUTSIDERS MAY THINK YOU'RE JUST PLAYING A GAME, BUT YOU AND I BOTH KNOW THE STAKES ARE MUCH HIGHER.

When the days are long, the players are grumbling, the parents and your athletic director seem to keep hounding you with questions and doubt, you haven't eaten supper at home in weeks, and the pressure feels like a weight on your shoulders, it's easy for frustration and doubt to creep in. It's easy to question, "Is this even worth it?"

That's when we need take a look back and remember our beginning ... the popping of the baseball into a glove and the crack of the bat. Remember your "why."

When wise college coaches recruit players, they not only search for good students and exceptionally skilled players, they're also attracted to players who play with passion and energy. The same applies to searching for coaches. I hired many assistant coaches in my day. While knowledge and experience are important, without passion and energy, skills aren't enough to inspire a team. As we advance in our coaching careers, it's important to remember what inspired us to first love the game.

I have either played or coached baseball most of my life. When I return to the small community where I grew up, I am thankful and reminded of the origin for my love for the game and the special way those beginnings inspired me to become a baseball lifer.

Pascal Mercier's quote says it best, "We leave something of ourselves behind when we leave a place, we stay there, even though we go away. And there are things in us that we can find again only by going back there."

It's difficult to have coaching success without passion. If you are tired, stressed, heavy, or feeling burnt out, start by going back to your roots. Ask yourself,

"When did I first realize that I loved baseball?"

"What inspired me to choose to pursue the game as far as my skills and abilities could take me?"

Passion and energy are contagious. Never hesitate to look back to the beginnings of your life in baseball. Let your love of the game rejuvenate you, energize you, and inspire you. Then it's time to look forward and ponder where a leadership role in baseball may take you.

Every good and perfect gift is from above, coming down from the Father of the heavenly lights, who does not change like shifting shadows.
—James 1:17

- 3 -

Know Where You're Heading
BUILDING A PERSONAL VISION

A vision is not just a picture of what could be; it is an appeal to our better selves, a call to be something more.
—*Rosabeth Moss Kanter*

YOU CAN'T HIT a target you can't see. Hall of famer Yogi Berra once said, "If you don't know where you're going, you might wind up someplace else." The future will arrive whether we are ready or not. It is critical to have a vision for our own career path as a coach.

My vision of the sport had always been to play Major League Baseball. My energy and focus were on "making it." There was no "Plan B." When my playing career officially ended, I'd only been attending Western Kentucky University one semester per year for 4 years. I missed everything about being on the field and the comradery of being a part of a team. Playing organized baseball had been a part of my life since I was eight years old and I was living without it for the first time. I needed to develop a new vision for my future.

To honor transparency, I'm not sure that I ever articulated the concept of building a vision as a 23-year-old, but I knew that I needed a plan. I started by focusing on finishing college and earning a degree.

Being out of the game only made my love and passion for baseball more apparent. So, I decided to pursue a career as a high school baseball coach. My cousin was teaching in the Polk County, Florida school system at the time, and suggested that Sharon and I make the move to central Florida. Suddenly, I was shifting from one vision to another.

The transition from playing at a high level to coaching high school athletes is not as easy as it may sound. I missed playing the game. Occasionally, I would play long toss with my players. After the break from competing, my damaged knee and shoulder felt better than they had felt in three years. Frequently, one of my players would say, "Coach, you're throwing great. You should try pro ball again." It's a good thing the movie *The Rookie* was a long way from being released, or I might have tried.

Not all baseball players are equipped to coach. There is a big difference in knowing how to play the game as opposed to knowing how to teach the skills, manage a game, and manage young players. Some elite college players and professionals never let go of that identity of being a player. It's painful to watch them enter the "real world." Without developing skills outside of playing baseball, it is very hard to adjust.

To be honest, fighting your way up the ladder to play in the majors is a selfish career. Your performance is up to your own effort. All eyes are on you. Even the trainers are there to take care of you.

Coaching is about as opposite as you can get—it's a selfless and often thankless job. Your success rests on how others perform. You are responsible for all the details no one sees (unless you make a mistake or what parents, fans, or your boss perceive is a mistake). Instead of being in the spotlight, you are leading and serving teenagers. Being responsible for others (especially teenagers) is vastly different than taking care of yourself.

My identity changed from a pitching prospect to a head coach at age 23. I can't honestly say that I never looked back at what might have been, but exchanging the glove for a clipboard was good for me.

There were challenges, of course, as a teacher in the high school classroom and on the field, but my purpose gradually became more defined. I soon became passionate about coaching young baseball players. It was a blast. The players made this challenge much easier for me.

When a person has purpose, it's much easier to begin thinking about a vision. Coaching at Lake Wales High School was the spark that inspired me to pursue a new career. In just a few years, this expanding vision would carry me back to my home state and coaching at the University of Kentucky.

Choose Your Compass

If you think about it, your personal vision is one of the most important things in your life. It's a compass that helps us determine if we're on track, otherwise we so easily wander—sometimes into great opportunities, and sometimes into regret.

Tommy Lasorda once said, "There are three types of people in baseball: Those who make it happen, those who watch it happen and those who wonder what happens." If we want to end our days feeling accomplished and satisfied that we've lived life on purpose, we've got to develop a vision for our lives.

In all your years of education, how many teachers, counselors, or professors ever asked you about your vision or helped you develop a personal mission statement? For me, the simple answer is zero. It's something that I loosely worked out for myself. But I believe there is a process we all go through, whether formally or not. The process involves identifying your passion, developing a plan of action, and finally pursuing your goals with both determination and patience.

Start With the Heart

As a high school student-athlete, if someone had asked me to name my goals for my life after high school, I would have listed them something like this:

1. Earn a scholarship to play basketball
2. Earn a scholarship to play baseball
3. Earn a degree from college

During my senior year in high school, my guidance counselor called me in to his office. He had looked at my grades, which were mediocre at best, and looked at my scores for the standardized test that all students took in that era. He told me he'd come up with the best-case scenario for me to earn a living after high school. Then he asked me if I had ever thought about being a fireman. I said, "No, I've never considered that."

He proceeded to tell me that college was probably not for me, and that Louisville was projected to have openings in their fire department. He said that I could be trained and have a good career as a fireman. Even then, I knew that being a fireman was a noble career—many young boys dreamed of driving those massive red fire trucks and saving people from danger. But sports had been my life, my dream, and my total vision. I left his office not knowing what to think or say.

My guidance counselor, without really knowing anything about my hopes and dreams, thought that being a fireman would be good for me. But I wanted to "throw heat," not put it out.

Within a few days I began thinking more seriously about what I wanted from life. This was the beginning of subconsciously developing a personal vision for my life. It wasn't yet on paper, but it was in my mind and in my heart.

The foundation of a vision starts with the heart:

What do you love to do?

What do you love to talk about?

What gives you a sense of fulfillment or satisfaction?

Be intentional about opening your heart to the vision that may be tucked away inside. Explore the possibilities and don't be dismayed if others don't see it yet.

A vision lives in our imagination. We see it when no one else sees it because it's still in our minds. A personal vision is a compelling idea for the future that is not quite yet in your grasp. It very well could be a part of God's plan for your life.

In his brilliant letter in the New Testament of the Bible, James wrote, *"Every good and perfect gift is from above, coming down from the Father of the heavenly lights, who does not change like shifting shadows"* (James 1:17).

God creates each one of us with talents, skills, and passions—good gifts meant to bring joy to our lives and make a difference in the world for others.

You and I are created on purpose for a purpose. We are not a mistake. The vision you have is not an accident—including your passion for baseball.

The game itself may not bring world peace, but I've seen it bring people together from every background, even different countries.

I've seen baseball teach young players how to work hard and believe in themselves, then go on to pass those gifts onto others.

Your desire to lead and coach isn't just a random pipe dream. It's a calling. If your personal vision includes God's will for your life and to make a positive impact on others, it is a gift from God.

> YOU AND I ARE CREATED ON PURPOSE FOR A PURPOSE. WE ARE NOT A MISTAKE. THE VISION YOU HAVE IS NOT AN ACCIDENT—INCLUDING YOUR PASSION FOR BASEBALL.

Find Out the Steps to Get There

Once we are honest about where we want to go, we can figure out what steps we can take to get there. Start by asking *how, who,* and *where*:

- How do I even get my foot in the door?
- Who is the best person to talk to about my personal vision?
- Where can I get started?

You don't need to have every step laid out, but you do need a rough idea. When I took my first job as a high school JV coach in Florida, I knew I wanted to pursue a head coaching position one day, but not quite yet. I was just smart enough to know that I was not ready to be the head coach yet. Sure, I knew how to play the game, but I didn't have the coaching tools. I had never led a group of any kind.

I set up a meeting with the head varsity coach, Joe Mangascle, and asked, "Joe, why don't you ask Mr. Mercer (our principal) if I can be your assistant?"

We had an assistant football coach that had been around for ten years or so. "Could he be the JV coach, and we can both help him as needed?" I asked. Joe liked the idea, so instead of becoming the head JV coach, I became the varsity assistant coach, learning from Coach Mangascle.

The following school year, Joe moved to a position in another town, and I became the head varsity coach. I couldn't have done an adequate job had I not worked under Joe the previous year.

Identify your vision and create a plan to get to where you want to go in life. It's very seldom ever too late.

Write Your Vision Statement

Your personal vision statement should tell your story and describe what you want for your future. Make it both bold and realistic. Then write it down on paper and keep it in front of you. This will keep it alive and more attainable.

As you clarify your personal vision for your life, consider the following:

- Know your desires, values, and passions.
- Consider how you will add value to others. This is vital to living with purpose.
- Take time to think it through and pray about it often.

Keep in mind, a mission statement is based on the present. A vision statement is about your future. It should be concise and easy to store in your mind and in your heart. It should be clear and inspirational.

Example A: "I want to be a transformational coach at the high school (or college) level known for his player-first competitive mentality, while teaching baseball skills and adding value to each player as an athlete and as a future husband, father, and citizen."

Example B: "I want to continue my career (as a developer, attorney, sales expert, craftsman, etc.), but I want to add value to others by investing time as a baseball coach, teaching young men the benefits of teamwork and competition."

One of my friends, Mike Linch, is a full-time pastor at a large church in the Atlanta area. He played college baseball and remains passionate about the game; he loves teaching and interacting with baseball players. Mike is the pitching coach at one of the public high schools in the Atlanta-area. Another friend, Kirk Hawkins, runs a successful video production company near St. Louis and is also an assistant coach at the high school level.

Scott Downs, one of my former players, pitched in the Major Leagues for 14 years and wanted to stay close to the game and help young players. He is in his third year as the head baseball coach at Lexington Catholic High School. Former Major League slugger Austin Kearns is a travel team coach and is making an impact on many young men. Teaching is great, but as you can see, it's not the only route to coaching.

If you are called to coach, whether it's college baseball, high school, travel ball, or youth league, find a way to make it happen. Craft a vision statement so that you can accomplish something special for yourself and for the young players you coach. The clarity can prevent you from spinning your wheels and flip flopping on your goals.

Invest in Your Future

Vision without character will have a bad ending. Surround yourself with positive people, men and women with integrity. Ken Blanchard once said, "Character—or lack of it—is still the nemesis of most leaders in our world today."

Many believe they can become effective leaders if they only gain the skills. Others believe they can become great leaders if they can just develop their character. Both are wrong. It takes skill *and* character.

Are you willing to make sacrifices for your vision? Achieving goals is never instant or easy. What are you willing to give up in order to fulfill the vision you have... golf, fishing, hunting, television? If your vision is big, bold, meaningful, and benefits others as well as your family and career, the sacrifices will be well worth it.

Imagine your life five years from now. Don't be afraid to think about your future self. Keeping your vision in front of you daily and taking the appropriate actions each day to encourage growth will place you in a great position to succeed.

> *"For I know the plans I have for you," declares the Lord, "plans to prosper you and not harm you, plans to give you hope and a future."*
> *—Jeremiah 29:11*

- 4 -

Know Your Identity

Whenever two people meet, there are really six people present. There is each man as he sees himself, each man as the other person sees him, and each man as he really is.
—William James

I WAS ON A Zoom call with almost one hundred baseball coaches and professional scouts recently. The topic of comparing came up and the leader asked me this question: "Keith, did you ever struggle with comparing yourself with others during your coaching career?"

I had to admit that there were occasions, especially early in my career, that I would glance into the opposing dugout and wonder if I needed to be more like that coach.

I'd see a great coach such as LSU's Skip Bertman and think, *Skip is such a great motivator and such a brilliant coach. I wish I could motivate my players in that way.*

Or I would see legendary Mississippi State University skipper Ron Polk and think, *Ron always has such a great practice plan, and he is so organized. His players are always so well-prepared and always seem to trust his plan. Perhaps I need to work harder on my practice organization.*

When our team competed against Hal Baird's Auburn team, I would wonder how Hal could be so relaxed and composed during a game while I was always on the top step of the dugout feeling the stress of every pitch.

Each of those coaches were uniquely gifted. They coached using their own strengths, personalities, and styles. We each bring our own strong suits to the table. If we compare too much, it becomes envy, and we then minimize the person God intended us to be. The key is to be able to learn from others without trying to be them. We each need to grow in our own identity.

In one respect, we may think of our identity as a combination of our DNA, where we were born, the culture and patterns passed down by our parents, and perhaps even the schools we attended. We may consider our faith (or the lack thereof) as part of who we are. We may look to our appearance, our friends, our win/loss record, or other achievements to answer the big question, "Who am I?"

> **WE CAN WASTE A LOT OF TIME ALLOWING OTHERS, OR OUR PAST, TO DICTATE WHO WE ARE.**

We can waste a lot of time allowing others, or our past, to dictate who we are. Listening to others—or even listening to that person we used to be—may impede our progress and prevent us from being who God created us to be.

How many times do we scroll through our social media feeds and compare ourselves to the coach who has come up with the latest, greatest hitting or pitching drill or philosophy? We compare ourselves to the coach who wows the media during the post-game press conference. It's easy to forget that we're only seeing a moment of their life, and it's a moment that highlights who they want us to believe they are.

The real question is, are we at peace with who we are, or do we simply cover our true selves with the insecurity of pretending to be someone else? Author Harper Lee wrote the statement, "Before I can live with other folks, I've got to live with myself. The one thing that doesn't abide by majority rule is a person's conscience."

Truthfully, our identity is a journey—and it isn't a sprint, but a marathon. We grow in our identity when we help others grow more positively in their own identities. Parents, teachers, coaches, and leaders in all walks of life have a tremendous opportunity to help others see in themselves their best identity.

Don't Believe in Lies

I don't think there's a person on this planet who doesn't wrestle with comparison and doubts from time to time. As we grow into our vision, we're going to be challenged. We'll hit roadblocks. Someone else will get the awards and accolades. Our identity should be based on something deeper if we're going to have the courage to soldier on.

I've been learning more about theologian Henri Nouwen's "Five Lies of Identity." Most of us can relate to being confronted with these lies and their false promises of fulfillment more often than we would care to admit. Using Nouwen's "lies" as a framework, let's take a look at each one and how coaches can stand up to them (comments next to the lies are mine):

1. I Am What I Do.

This may be the most challenging lie for coaches, perhaps even more than for men and women of other professions. After all, we're competitive by nature. As a coach, what happens when we get too old to swing a fungo, throw batting practice, or even demonstrate how to do a specific skill? Who are we when we lose our position in the dugout? We may still be called "coach" but that isn't who we are.

We each must accept that coaching is never who we are, but only what we do as a living or a calling. Please know this—you are infinitely more than anything you could ever do or produce. As coaches, we are to compete well and give our best effort, but in the end, our work does not define who we are. We are more than a title.

2. I Am What I Have.

The trophies you collect over your career will not define who you are. Your bank account, where you live, and vehicles you drive also do not define who you are. What happens when people forget how many games you have won, or if your money disappears?

No, you are more than wins and losses, and you are much more than what you possess.

3. I Am What Others Say or Think of Me.

Opinions come and go. When you win, people may say good things about you. When you lose, they will say negative things about you. But, seriously, have you changed? No, absolutely not. You are the same person; your family and true friends still love and admire you.

It's easier said than done, but it is always wise to ignore social media and sports talk show hosts after a loss or a disappointing season. The people who post and respond go the way of the wind. Those are not the people you want shaping your identity.

4. I Am Nothing More Than My Worst Moment.

A failure is an event. It is not who you are as a person. Coaches cannot control every detail of every game. As hard as we may try, we can't control a hitter's swing. We can't throw strikes for the pitcher. We can't stay down for an infielder on a ground ball. We can't hit the cutoff man for our outfielders, and we can't make the right calls for the umpires.

As a coach, you've probably made some bonehead moves. You may have even put the wrong player in the lineup or left your starting pitcher in too long, but that doesn't mean that your motive or your heart was wrong. Your significance and who you are in God's eyes are so special that not even the worst failure or the most horrendous loss can affect who you are to Him. This moment will pass, and if you exercise wisdom, you will learn from the mistakes you may have made.

5. *I Am Nothing Less Than My Best Moment.*

Even your best win and your best decision, as great as they are and as good as they may feel, are still external. They are not who you are. Enjoy the good moments. Work hard for them; but life teaches us to "make hay in the sunshine and play in the rain."

Celebrate the victories, learn from the losses, and remain steady. Many times, your staff and team will emulate your emotions. Coaches are leaders and leaders must be able to exude steadiness and trustworthiness. You are more than anything good you can do on your best day. You are more than what you do, say, or accomplish.

***

It's easy to fall into the trap of taking every loss, and win, personally. I have often felt coaches receive too much credit for a win or a successful season and too much blame for a loss or a disappointing season. Of course, when the losses come, coaches should embrace "the buck stops here" mentality. Having said that, there are usually factors out of a coach's control that may or may not determine the outcome of a game.

A coach can make every right move and place his team in a position to win, but a coach can't control a hard-hit line drive into the glove of a leaping shortstop, a rain delay which ends the starting pitcher's day prematurely, an injury that takes your best player out of the lineup, or a blown call by an umpire. But a coach can control how he or she responds to the situation.

We can take the high road. Be confident in who you are as a coach and as a person. Just don't expect to find a sympathetic ear after a loss. Outside of a coach's immediate family, sympathy doesn't usually exist. Businessmen will not receive a pat on the back when the company loses money. Coaches won't get encouraging words after a losing season, and many times even after a winning season.

One year while coaching at Kentucky, we won thirty-eight games, finished fourth out of twelve in the most competitive league in the country, and yet, we did not receive an at-large NCAA tournament bid from the selection committee. When I complained to my athletic director, he simply said, "Win more games next season." Lesson learned, don't expect sympathy from anyone—if you don't have thick skin, you'll develop it. Let resiliency be your defining attribute.

Winning doesn't necessarily make you a winner. Losing doesn't make a coach a loser. Honestly, I have led teams to wins that we should have lost. We sometimes get a break and win even when the other team performs better. Does that loss make the coach on a team that performed well a loser? I think not. Our identity should be more about the way we prepare and coach our athletes and the character we exude, win or lose.

Many people consider Abraham Lincoln one of our greatest presidents. Did you know, he lost almost every political race before he was elected president? Was he a winner before he became president? Of course, he was. Don't get me wrong, winning is fun and we should always, without question, compete to win. But our identity should be built upon effort, preparation, the way we treat others, resiliency, and integrity.

Look Up

When I see my identity horizontally, I am always left wanting. Comparison has always been an enemy of individuals, but with the advent of social media it may now be the biggest enemy of all.

When I choose to see my identity vertically, I understand that God knows my weaknesses and failures. On my worst day, He still loves me and calls me His child. He even encourages me to come to Him when I'm having one of those days. The well-known parable of the Prodigal Son (Luke 15:11–32) is a classic example of God running to us on our worst day. If you want to know how you compare, look up. You are the apple of His eye.

The ultimate mystery of our lives may be God's unconditional love for us. *"See what great love the Father has lavished on us, that we should be called children of God! And that is what we are!"* (1 John 3:1a).

I love the quote by William James at the beginning of this chapter, but please allow me to alter the quote because there are really *eight* people present: all those James mentioned and, more importantly, the way God sees us and the way we perceive Him.

Whatever good we may accomplish, we do with the gifts God has given us. We should strive to be good stewards of those gifts. And, whether we are disappointed in our losses or celebrating our wins, it is good to remember what Saint Francis of Assisi once said: "I am who I am in the sight of God, nothing more, nothing less."

For the Lord does not see as man sees: man looks on the outward appearance, but the Lord looks on the heart.
—1 Samuel 16:7b

- 5 -

Take Your Team
DEVELOPING A VISION FOR YOUR PROGRAM

*People buy into the leader before
they buy in to their vision.
—John Maxwell*

EARLY IN MY career at the University of Kentucky, I encountered the new and exciting challenge of developing a vision for the Wildcat baseball program. My first few years were consumed with recruiting and learning how to manage a Division I program while balancing life as a husband and a new dad.

We were the only school in our league without a full allotment of scholarships. We had no indoor facilities, and we were the northern-most school in the SEC. Building a successful program seemed like a daunting challenge, but I was 26 years old and very competitive—and I had inherited a veteran team that was hungry to win.

In the first year, we turned it around and finished second in the Eastern Division of the league with one hand tied behind our backs! We didn't whine about our situation. We had a vision for our program, and we went to work.

First, my assistant coach, John Butler, and I secured part time jobs to supplement our incomes. Then, we got permission from a horse sales pavilion to put up batting cages and built two dirt mounds for our pitchers.

We hit fungos in the stall area and practiced baserunning there, as well. There was no heat in the large horse barn but at least we were out of the elements. We even made use of the chairback seats in the pavilion when we held a baseball clinic fundraiser. I still remember former big leaguers Jim Kaat and Russ Nixon, along with active Major League infielder Doug Flynn, speaking at our clinic there.

Within just a few years, the budget and the facilities began to improve. Without a vision, a strong work ethic, and talented, competitive players, we would have always been victims of our situation instead of winners.

Cast the Vision

One day after the players and coaches left the field following practice, I found myself sitting on some old bleachers on the first base side of what was known in those days as Shively Field. This was during my third or fourth year at Kentucky. I was thinking about all the work to be done and about our recruiting needs. Our playing field, seating area, press box, and locker rooms were sub-par, to say the least. Consequently, we had to put a lot of effort into the recruiting process.

We had a chain link fence in the outfield and all along the perimeter of the field. We had three sets of wooden bleachers and a small concrete block building that served as a storage area on the first floor and a press box on the second floor. This press box wasn't even behind home plate! It was situated behind the wooden bleachers parallel to the first base line and it could barely seat six people.

The grass on the field was very thick Kentucky Bluegrass. It was beautiful... but not conducive for SEC baseball. Our infielders charged everything aggressively and a hard-hit groundball would quickly become routine in the thick grass. Our grounds crew also maintained the football practice fields, the football stadium field, and the track area. They were limited in numbers and time. So, my assistant and I quickly learned the fine art of field maintenance. Shively Field and its dugouts, bleachers, and overall ambience was severely lacking for a Division I baseball program. The challenges were clear.

As I sat there in the bleachers contemplating the work ahead of me, I allowed my mind to wonder. Just a few years earlier, Coach Butler and I had been graduate assistants at Mississippi State. They had a *real* stadium and an extremely well-maintained Bermuda grass field. As I physically relaxed in the bleachers, my mind was swirling like an old-fashioned butter churn. I was dreaming about what "could be" at Shively Field.

After several minutes of daydreaming, two of my better pitchers came by the field to pick up something one had left. They saw me all alone and sauntered over to my spot in the bleachers.

One pitcher, Jay Ray, asked, "Coach, what are you doing here? Practice was over an hour ago."

"Well, I'm not getting much field work done, but I'm thinking about some changes I would like to make here in our facility," I replied.

Jeff Hellman, the other player, then asked me a question that took my "dreaming" from wishful thinking to the beginning of a solid vision for our program.

"Coach, where do you see the facilities and the program five years from now?" asked Jeff.

I was only about 29 years old at the time, so five years seemed like a long time to wait for anything. But I answered as if I had written it down as a part of a vision statement. That was interesting because I don't think I knew what a vision statement was when I was 29 years old.

I told him that I expected the Wildcats to take the next step up from being a good SEC team to a consistent NCAA tournament participant. I also shared with them plans for chairback seats, season ticket sales, a real press box, adding lights, and a better playing surface. I also planned to take recruiting to a new level.

I told the two young righties that it started with them, and that they would be a part of building something special.

We reached most of those goals in less than five years. A crucial part of the process is that I had verbalized a huge part of my vision to two players that I respected. They became a part of my vision.

Soon after, I shared this vision with my staff, athletic director, donors, and fans. Winning helped, for sure, but sharing the vision helped us all stay motivated and locked into what we wanted to accomplish as a staff and a team.

Roll Up Your Sleeves

A compelling vision stirs the passion within us. It lets people know where we are going and where we want to take them, if they'll join us.

During that era, our administration wasn't ready or willing to help with the vision, so I would ask my AD, "If I raise the money will you pay for half?" The administration would usually agree to that, but sometimes I would be left with the responsibility of raising the entire amount of whatever project that would enhance our program and help in recruiting.

When it comes to your vision for the program, don't take "no" for an answer (in a respectful way). You must say "yes" to yourself, be willing to roll up your sleeves, and not let anything get in the way of your vision.

Along the way, it will be tweaked, improved, and carried along with a team of believers: players, staff, donors, fans, friends, and administrators. Perhaps not all of them at once, but that's okay. The key word in the previous sentence is *team*. If you attempt major projects without support from a team, expect burnout to be the major obstacle.

Solomon, wisely wrote in Ecclesiastes 4:9–10, *"Two are better than one, because they have a good reward for their labor. If either of them falls down, one can lift the other up. But pity anyone who falls and has no one to help them up."* A dynamic vision is normally too large for one to carry. We need help.

Of course, a bold vision for your program or organization is much more than facilities. For college coaches, it includes recruiting talented players. At all levels it should include developing a winning coaching philosophy and a plan to bring out the best in each player.

I appreciate how Simon Sinek explains the importance of knowing both your "why" in life and having a vision. "They're equally as important. They're different things," he says. "Why comes from the past. It's an origin story, it's where we come from." However, vision is about the future. "Vision is where we are going ... it's the world you're trying to build," he says, and it's more than a goal to obtain, "I

> WE NEED TO KNOW BOTH THE WHY THAT DRIVES US AND WHAT CAUSE WE ARE WORKING TOWARD.

call it a just cause." We need to know both the why that drives us and what cause we are working toward.

My "why" in coaching is that I not only have always loved baseball, but, more importantly, I loved the players who played baseball. My vision as a coach was to build a competitive, winning program for players to thrive and grow, while at the same making the administration, alumni, and fans proud.

How your team represents your school or organization should be a huge part of the vision you have. In many cases, athletic teams are the most visible representatives of a school. A significant part of your vision for your program should take into consideration that the name on the front of the jersey goes with you wherever you compete.

Look For Examples

Not all coaches are visionaries, but all coaches need to have a vision. You don't necessarily need to create or build a vision from scratch. Consider the vision of coaches you admire and then adopt the concepts within them.

There are certain coaches who have impressive coaching trees with a long line of assistants who go on to become head coaches. I think of Skip Bertman (LSU), Jack Legget (Clemson), and Ron Polk (Mississippi State). Each of those coaches have had numerous assistants earn success as head coaches at other schools. You can be sure that parts of their vision and philosophy have been used in multiple programs. Whether the former assistant coaches originated the concepts within their program vision isn't that important. What is important is that athletes from dozens of schools are benefitting. The vision is bigger than any individual.

The more coaches you listen to and the more leaders you follow, the bigger the chance is that something they say will resonate with you. Attend clinics, listen to podcasts, and read books. Not everything that is said will touch you, but you will know it when something does. Bring those ideas and concepts into your program as a part of your vision.

Define the Destination

A good vison defines the destination and the values that will bring pride to the organization or school. An effective vision provides a connection between today and tomorrow and should energize and motivate those involved. It should involve future success and set a standard of excellence. Be both bold and realistic.

It's important to clarify your vision and it's vital that it adds value to others. It's crucial for everyone involved to understand the "why" behind it and how it will bring satisfaction and value to all. It's more than just a goal to check off; that's why Sinek called it a "just cause."

Write it on paper and post it in the locker room and dugout. This will help the vision become even more alive and accessible to everyone on the team. But don't get distracted if someone doesn't buy into your vision. We live in an imperfect world. Learn from those who don't grasp your vision. Perhaps you can tweak your vision or articulate it in a better way. Oftentimes, actions speak louder than words.

As a leader, you see the vision first, so it doesn't become real to others until you start moving forward. Once you do, others will catch the vision and follow. Also, in most cases, resources from donors and your administration are contingent on movement towards implementing your plan. The movement will most likely include winning! So don't let the peripheral goals get in the way of what you were hired to do on the field.

Bring in the Team

One of the biggest mistakes a coach or leader can make is to assume that everyone knows your vision and clearly understands it. I have made this mistake before. Make sure that you articulate your vision to everyone who will participate in helping it come to fruition. Those following you must understand exactly where you want to go and how tremendously beneficial it will be to everyone in the program.

Great teams make everything look easy—but it's never easy. Nothing worthwhile ever is.

It's pouring excellence into the little things that we do each day. Some of the things athletes and coaches work on every day is never seen, but all these moments in practice work together towards success.

Coach, you need to communicate to your team that what they're doing day in and day out is impacting what they want to accomplish. Don't assume they just know it. Recognize and celebrate how players contribute to the vision each day. Success is a team effort from everyone: coaches, players, parents, managers, administrators, donors, and fans. When any of them give time, effort, or financial support, let them know they are a contributing to the program's vision.

No one wants to follow a leader with a small vision. Competitive people want to be challenged. Create a big vision and do something daily to implement it.

Your vision should be the GPS of your program. The program will hit some rough patches and will encounter setbacks but keep your eye on the prize. Stay focused and determined. Even if you fall short at times, you will accomplish much more if you spend time building a vision for your program. The fun part will be watching your vision come to life.

Where there is no vision, the people perish.
—Proverbs 29:18a KJV

PART 2:
SECOND BASE

Build Alignment

- 6 -

Turning Vision into Reality

*Leaders have three fundamental responsibilities:
They craft a vision, they build alignment,
and they champion execution.*
—The Work of Leaders *by Julie Straw, Barry Davis,
Mark Scullard, and Susie Kukkonen*

A HITTER CAN HAVE the most beautiful swing since Ken Griffey Jr., but if he can't square up the ball it's useless.

A pitcher can have perfect mechanics and throw 95 mph, but if he can't throw strikes he won't be on the mound when the umpire says, "Play ball!"

A coach can have a great vision and a solid coaching philosophy, but if he can't connect with the players, he'll never see that vision become reality. Connecting is crucial.

Players want to learn. They want to be inspired. It's important for a coach to be able to touch each player in a way that will motivate them to play well and give their best effort. The way a coach speaks to his team and talks to each individual player is a craft that needs to be worked on frequently. As a coach, you want to be able to pour into your players' games and, more importantly, into their lives.

I could always tell when I was reaching my players. It's a great feeling when you see them "get it." It's discouraging when they don't. If your message confuses a player or goes over his head, that's on you as a coach. That's why coaches need to constantly work on the art of communicating with the team and with each individual player.

It's Not One-Size-Fits-All

I played for dozens of coaches and managers throughout my playing career. Most of them were knowledgeable about baseball. I'm sure they all loved the game. But to some, I was just another pitcher in the bullpen. The leaders who had the greatest impact were the few who communicated with me and chose to develop a relationship with me.

The top of the list was Jack Lamabe, my pitching coach when I was playing in the Expos organization. Jack had pitched several years in the big leagues and had great stories. He simplified and improved my pitching mechanics and talked about setting up hitters and competing. Perhaps most importantly, Jack was an intentional listener.

Occasionally, Jack would simply say, "Madison, let's go down to the bullpen and have a chat." He'd talk pitching, then ask me a couple of questions and listen. Sometimes he'd recall a story from his days as a player, then ask me another question or two, and again, listen. Jack had a way of making me feel comfortable as a player.

Despite our differences—I was a 19-year-old southern country boy, and he was a middle-aged man from Massachusetts—he always found ways to connect. I believe he truly valued what I had to say. Ironically, we eventually coached against each other near the beginning of my career at Kentucky. Jack coached at LSU for a couple of years after a successful career as a professional player and coach.

Russ Nixon was one of my all-time favorite managers. Russ was a former Major League catcher, so he knew pitching and pitchers well. He carried himself with a strong confidence. I admired the old-school toughness, but also his honesty and the way he treated players.

One night, I had a rough outing on the mound. I knew that pitchers were always one start or one relief appearance from being demoted or released. I took my poor performance seriously. The next day before we dressed for the game, Russ called me into his tiny office in Al Lopez Stadium in Tampa. I didn't know which direction the conversation might go.

Russ was direct, "Keith, you obviously didn't have your best stuff last night and your control was horse ****.

You had a rough night on the mound, but you are my closer. If I call on you tonight, I know you will not let us down. I believe in you." I walked out of his office feeling confident and I finished strong that summer.

Jack Lamabe and Russ Nixon had different leadership styles—in fact, they were almost opposites in the way they communicated with me—yet they were both effective. There's no one-size-fits-all in coaching communication. Alignment begins when we focus on leading with respect, building rapport, and creating a culture of poise under pressure.

> ALIGNMENT BEGINS WHEN WE FOCUS ON LEADING WITH RESPECT, BUILDING RAPPORT, AND CREATING A CULTURE OF POISE UNDER PRESSURE.

Lead with Respect

One of the greatest ways we can show and earn respect is through listening.

We can't fake listening. It shows in our body language and especially in our eyes. We've all been there when we're trying to talk to someone only to watch their eyes search the room for someone more interesting to talk to. This is disrespect. If you want your players to listen, start by listening to them.

It's not easy when you've got more things to do than hours in your day. Listening takes time and intentionality. As coaches, we're used to talking and giving instructions.

It takes humility and selflessness to stop your agenda and truly tune in to what someone else has to say. Marketing guru Dean Jackson says it this way: "Listening is an art that requires attention over talent, spirit over ego, others over self."

Every player will communicate with you—either through words or body language. Often, players are intimidated and choose not to speak with their coach. When they do, it's usually either important or a cry for attention. Listening is often the only thing needed to help someone. It demonstrates to your player that what he has to say is important and that he is valuable to the team.

It's okay to set boundaries for talking. We've all had that player who interrupts during practice or a meeting. Kindly and firmly asking them to have the conversation after practice not only gets practice back on track, but also demonstrates respect for all the players and their practice time. You're modeling how and when to be heard.

A Foundation of Rapport

During my first two years of coaching at Lake Wales High School, I was definitely a novice in the art of communication. I had just gotten out of pro ball, and I had a lot to learn. But I was building rapport with my players without even knowing it.

Off the field I talked to them about fishing, their families, girlfriends, grades, music, and their favorite MLB team. All of the genuine non-baseball conversations helped them to feel more comfortable with me, and to be honest, helped me feel both comfortable and confident in helping them on the field.

As I moved into coaching college ball, the dynamic shifted. College guys were looking for independence and my playing years were farther behind me. But I still wanted to be approachable and in sync with our players. I had to be more creative in establishing a rapport with them.

Coaching is so much more rewarding when you have a satisfying rapport with your players. When a coach can demonstrate that the player is important by listening attentively, exuding positive body language, and creating a genuine atmosphere, effective coaching will be the result.

The non-verbal aspect of communicating may be as important as the expertise a coach imparts on a player. A coach may have excellent knowledge and use the most effective drills, but success will be limited if he can't get the best out of his players.

In my first year of coaching at Kentucky, I inherited a team that had just broken the school record for losses. Instead of going into the situation looking to get rid of players on a losing team, I decided to make a goal of helping the players returning from that disappointing season get better.

I'm so glad I didn't clean house. Some of the best people I've ever met were from that team. And they were talented players; they just needed encouragement, enthusiasm, and empathy. In just one season, the same group of players went from a losing team to breaking the school record for wins. The veteran players on that team helped me in my role as a very young head coach in the SEC. I had a blast helping them leave Kentucky as winners.

Effective coaches lead with empathy, not ultimatums. Simon Sinek wisely observed that business leaders can be so quick to hire and fire. "You can't hire and fire your children...," he says, "So, why is it when somebody has performance problems...our instinct is to say, 'You're out.' We do not practice empathy." Empathy, says Sinek, starts by asking, "Are you okay? I'm worried about you. What's going on?"

> **EFFECTIVE COACHES LEAD WITH EMPATHY, NOT ULTIMATUMS.**

If a player isn't performing, it's the coach's responsibility to find out why his athlete isn't measuring up. It's your job, coach, to help the player feel comfortable talking to you. This is the beginning of the communication process that will help him turn failure into success.

Life is more than baseball. Do you know what's going on in your player's life? Is one of his parents sick, or are they getting a divorce? Are his grades slipping? Or did his girlfriend drop him like a hot potato? Empathy is being concerned about the player as a person, not just his performance.

Instead of saying, "Hey, you've made three errors in the last two games. If you don't improve, I'll be finding a new infielder!" the empathetic coach says, "You've made three errors in the last two games, what's going on with you? I'm here to help."

Genuine answers will come when you've built genuine connections. Sometimes the best connections begin when working with a small group of players: focused sessions in the bullpen, hitting fungos before or after practice, talking about music or family on the bus. You build trust when you ask them how their day is going and then actually wait for the answer.

It's so important to learn and appreciate what your players value. This takes some effort. Look for clues for what is important to them. Most players obviously value their families. It's one thing to ask a player how they are doing, it's another level of caring when you say, "Jeremy, I know your little sister was competing in the regional volleyball championship yesterday, how did her team do?" When a coach communicates at that level, a genuine connection can be developed.

Oftentimes the coach's office can be mistaken for the principal's office. Catch players after practice and ask, "What did you see in practice today?" Or set up a meeting at a coffee shop.

Coaching is more than X's and O's—it's building a culture of trust so you can bring out the best in your team. Ask your players real questions, smart questions. Limit the small talk and get to the things that matter in a player's development and his life.

Players learn much from knowledgeable coaches who choose to spend time with them and get to know them. And when the time comes for you to make game-time decisions, you'll be a step ahead when you know your players.

Keep Your Poise Under Pressure

The most difficult thing to do in sports may be to hit a small white ball traveling 90 mph and spinning 33 times per second. It's a tough thing to do! It takes focus, composure, and inner strength. Being mentally tough may be the difference between average and good, or good and great.

If you want to lead a winning program, you need to have the same mental toughness you expect from your players. Your team will only be as mentally tough as you are.

Can you keep your poise under pressure? Fans love to see a temper tantrum from the coach. They'll talk for days about the coach who lost his mind. To be honest, players often get fired up watching their coach, too. After all, the "passion" and fire in a tantrum must show how much you care as you stand up for your team. Or does it?

As you "stand up" for your team, are you in control of the situation? Or does the situation control you?

A few years ago, I was watching a college football game where it seemed like the visiting team was getting every break. The home team had fallen behind just before half-time. The momentum was definitely against them.

The home team had possession of the ball and on third down the quarterback kept looking to the sideline. I'm sure he was hoping to find a little support, maybe a, "We've got this." Instead, the offensive coordinator and the head coach were both ranting. Red-faced, they charged up and down the sideline screaming at officials and anyone that crossed their path.

Meanwhile, the quarterback was trying to maintain his composure, but he needed help. He received none. The coaching staff was out of control and in no place to offer instruction, let alone encouragement. The game was on the line and he was on his own.

In front of 70,000 fans, national TV, and a motivated opponent, the quarterback attempted to right the ship himself. Eventually, he and the team lost.

Coach, you can be passionate *and* poised. Be competitive. Be

> YOU CAN BE PASSIONATE *AND* POISED. BE COMPETITIVE. BE EMOTIONAL IF YOU MUST. EXUDE ENERGY, FOR SURE. BUT FOR THE SAKE OF YOUR ATHLETES, BE IN CONTROL.

emotional if you must. Exude energy, for sure. But for the sake of your athletes, be in control.

Your hitters are watching. If you want them to be focused against that pitcher everyone fears, show them how to do it. Model self-control. Practice composure. Build your own tools for mental toughness before you expect it from your team.

When the going gets tough, take the focus off of yourself and do what you were hired to do: coach, instruct, strategize, compete, and build your players up. It's not about you. There are times we must minimize our ego and our frustration—even our anger at the officials—and just coach. Expect excellence from your players. Make strategic moves. And most of all, believe in your players.

There are lots of coaching styles and philosophies. I'm not saying you need to coach in just one way. But are you being intentional in how you listen and model respect? Are you leading by example? If you want your players to hear what you have to say, you have to build rapport first.

> *My dear brothers and sisters, take note of this: Everyone should be quick to listen, slow to speak and slow to become angry.*
> *—James 1:19*

- 7 -

Communication

The interesting thing about coaching is that you have to trouble the comfortable and comfort the troubled.
—Ric Charlesworth

ONE SUMMER, I was asked to be the baseball guy at a well-known sports camp in the mountains of North Carolina. The terrain of the camp was not conducive to baseball, so a city park was secured for our practices. It was a three or four mile drive down the steep, curvy, narrow highway to the baseball complex in the valley.

As we drove down the mountain for our first practice, I noticed that the players were unusually quiet for a group of teenagers. Being from all over the South, Midwest, and East Coast, they didn't really know each other. I was sure that once we got on the baseball field they would connect.

Except for the warning of rattlesnakes recently seen on the field and in a dugout, the baseball skills and teaching portion of the camp went very well. It helped that I had recently retired Major League catcher Eddie Taubensee helping!

At the end of the day, it was time to make the trek back up the mountain. The guys were somewhat chattier and a little smellier on the bus ride back to camp headquarters. As I looked back, I noticed two guys sitting in the middle who seemed unusually quiet. They wore the same high school baseball t-shirts, so I assumed they came to the camp together. I decided to go back in the bus and get better acquainted with them. I wanted to see why they seemed to be a bit unhappy.

"Hey, where are you guys from?" I asked as I sat in the seat in front of them.

The boys told me their school, confirming they did come together.

"Good program. I've recruited a few players from your school in the past," I replied. Then I asked about their coach, who was well-known in their state.

"I hate that guy!" one of the players immediately blurted out.

I was stunned but decided to dig a little deeper. "I've got to ask, why do you dislike your coach so much?"

"At practice, every time I make a mistake, instead of teaching me, he makes fun of me and makes me feel stupid," answered the same young player.

I asked the other player how he felt about his coach: "I feel the same way. Sometimes I think I never want to go to practice again."

I apologized and told these two young baseball players to never give up on their dream; I assured them that this camp would be a fun and learning environment.

When I got home from camp I did a little more research on this program. After all, I'd recruited talented players from the team. I found that the coach's success wasn't from his ability to lead and teach skills, but instead came from inheriting talented players from a phenomenal youth league program that fed this high school year after year.

For weeks I thought about these two players from camp who were filled with potential yet ready to give up on the game. Thousands of players hang up their gloves every year. How many of them quit because they feel beaten down or belittled?

Coaches, we have the opportunity to fan the flame of passion for America's pastime or take a fire hose and drench the spark that burns in the heart of up-and-coming players. It all comes down to communication.

Words are seeds that do more than blow around.
They land on our hearts and not on the ground.
Be careful what you plant and be careful what you say.
You might have to eat what you planted someday.

This anonymous poem says it well—are you going to want to eat what you're planting?

Learning to communicate was key to my success and amassing 850 wins over 28 years of coaching high school and college ball. Baseball is a team sport. You cannot win alone. You might have a lucky streak or catch a ride on the coattails of a program that feeds you good players. But if you want to build a successful career, you have to communicate to build and inspire.

Teach Clearly

It's easy to throw out a ton of information at your players. After all, once the season starts, there's not a lot of time for practice between all the games. But too much talk often creates more confusion than convincing.

Define Your Terms

Make sure your athletes understand your terminology. Baseball is a sport steeped in tradition, but the lingo is ever evolving. In recent years, analytics has contributed to changing the way coaches communicate with players. Fancy metrics and words will only help if everyone is on the same page with how you use them.

Slow Down

We need to slow the game down for players so that they can perform at the highest level. I've watched coaches talk non-stop during a game. How much does a player hear when a fastball with movement is what he needs to focus on?

As Yogi Berra famously said, "You can't think and hit at the same time." Baseball is a reaction game. During a game, a player will not remember the 20 points of hitting. If he's lucky, he may remember one or two.

Plan Your Practice

Make practice time count. Get good at planning practices with effective drills that build progressive skills. When a player is coached well and practices well, a quality performance during the game will become instinctive.

When I was a graduate assistant coach under Ron Polk at Mississippi State, I learned the value of posting practice plans. First, it holds you accountable to be prepared. Second, you're modeling the importance of details. Do you want your players to be disciplined and attentive during practice? Model intentionality and preparation.

Third, and most importantly, it helps players get mentally prepared for what they're going to be working on that day. Your players can't meet your expectations if they don't know what you expect of them.

Set Them Up for Success

There are other ways to reach players. Some of them seem insignificant, but in my view they are important.

For instance, when you bring in a group of players or the entire team for a short meeting during practice, make sure they are not facing the sun. It's hard for a player to make eye contact and pay attention if he has to cover his eyes to protect them from the sun.

Another small but important thing; if you have something very important to share with the team, make sure that you share it while the players are fresh. If you share the info at the end of a demanding practice, they are much less likely to grasp what you are saying. They've been in class all day; players (and coaches) are tired and hungry at the end of practice.

If your players aren't getting it, develop applicable drills or learn to teach fundamentals in a new way. Many times, just explaining a technique using different words or with a bit more enthusiasm will allow the light to come on for a player.

Be creative in your approach to coaching. Practice with precision. Game time will bring out what you've put in.

Speak to Build Up

One winter night I was sitting on my sofa watching a college basketball game when the camera panned to a closeup of the coach "correcting" a player on the bench. It was easy to read

> **IN WHAT OTHER PROFESSION IS IT ACCEPTABLE FOR A MIDDLE-AGED MAN TO CURSE AND SCREAM AT A YOUNG MAN ON NATIONAL TV? OR ANYWHERE, FOR THAT MATTER.**

the coach's lips—words I won't repeat here. The young player in his late teens sat stoic and simply took it from the coach. The scene was awkward for me to watch; I couldn't imagine how the player must have felt.

I couldn't stop thinking about the incident. As I processed it later that night, I couldn't help but think to myself, *In what other profession is it acceptable for a middle-aged man to curse and scream at a young man on national TV? Or anywhere, for that matter.*

Let that sink in a minute. Where else in the professional world is this behavior from a leader okay?

Sure, the coach may have gotten his point across, but at what cost? And why is this acceptable in athletics? Should coaches be more like a Marine drill instructor or a compassionate teacher? There are times, because of attitude or poor effort, a coach needs to get a player's attention. Just make sure he knows why he is being disciplined, and don't forget to let him know that you want the best for him and for the team.

Coaches take extreme liberties at times when correcting a player's mental or physical mistakes. Cursing, name calling, sarcasm, and cynicism are all demeaning and humiliating for players. Put-downs are never a winning way to communicate.

Whether you're a person of faith or not, the Bible has a lot of good principals. For me, it's the North Star, the ultimate play book. Now don't get me wrong, I know there are a lot of "Christians" who haven't been an example of what the Bible teaches. But that doesn't mean the principals are wrong.

The apostle Paul was one of those. He had been one of the biggest persecutors of early Christians. Historians believe he stood by and held the cloaks of the men who stoned Stephan to death. Paul's mission was to silence those who talked about Jesus's life, death, and resurrection, until he encountered Jesus's grace and love for himself. He knew the Holy Scriptures before; he became passionate about living and leading with God's love after.

In Ephesians 4:29, Paul tells us to watch what we say and how we say it. *"Do not let any unwholesome talk come out of your mouths, but only what is helpful for building others up according to their needs, that it may benefit those who listen."*

We often talk about what *not* to do—the "unwholesome" talk like swearing or crude joking. But how much do we focus on what *to* do—building others up.

> **REMEMBER, WE DON'T COACH BASEBALL. WE COACH BASEBALL PLAYERS.**

Remember, we don't coach baseball. We coach baseball players.

It's our job to lead, guide, and speak clearly and constructively to those in our charge. It's our job to be poised and to be there for our players. Without instruction and encouragement, you're not really coaching.

We Get What We Speak

Players are going to live up or down to the expectations we set. The less we expect from them, the less they give. Expect more, get more.

When I was playing professional baseball, I would overhear coaches say things like, "His hands are not soft," or, "He can't throw strikes," or, "He can't hit the off-speed pitch." Coaches and scouts tend to label an athlete, but what they're really doing is limiting him.

I would watch certain players spend weeks, months, and even their whole careers trying to shake a label. No matter how they played and improved, the label would stick because a coach didn't take the time to notice, or a scout didn't want to be proven wrong. As a coach, I wanted to learn from that.

What we give our attention to grows.

Ken Blanchard says it this way: "The more attention you pay to a behavior, the more it will be repeated. Accentuating the positive and redirecting the negative are the best tools for increasing productivity."

Most coaches are excellent at catching players doing something wrong. How good are we at catching them doing something right?

I'm not saying we should praise players just for the sake of

> **IF WE FOCUS MORE ON CONSTRUCTIVE FEEDBACK, WE'RE GOING TO SET AN EXPECTATION OF GROWTH.**

it. But if we focus more on constructive feedback, we're going to set an expectation of growth.

People feel good when they make positive gains. They're motivated to keep working when they make improvements. They gain a sense of belonging when they know their efforts are seen as contributing to the team. They begin to see themselves as winners and rise to the expectation.

Pick the moment you see improvement in a specific skill your athlete has been working on and make your praise specific.

Saying, "Nice pitch," is fine, but the more specifically you describe what an individual is doing correctly, the more lasting and effective your feedback will be.

"That grip you've been working on with your changeup has made such a difference in the deception of the pitch and in your command of the pitch. Keep working on that. It's going to win for you." That's specific encouragement.

When you give specific feedback, your athletes know what to focus on and what to keep doing. Plus, they hear that you believe in them. Sincere, deserved encouragement is a powerful tool—it will win for you.

Talk About What a Player Can Do

During the late '80s, we had the daunting task of playing Auburn University in the SEC tournament. Their best hitter was Frank Thomas. Actually, he was the best hitter in college baseball at the time.

During this particular game, it was in the late innings and we had a one run lead with two outs. Auburn had loaded bases with big Frank Thomas coming to the plate. A base hit could put them in the lead. Frank could hit just about any pitch thrown ... very hard.

I brought in my closer, Steve Culkar. Before I left the mound, I told him, "Steve, you have one spot to locate your fastball in order to get Thomas out. I know you can do this... that's why I brought you in. You have a good fastball, and you have the ability to locate it. The only place you can throw your fastball is right under his hands."

What I *didn't* say, is, "You throw very hard, but you don't get a lot of movement. If you miss anywhere out over the plate, the game is over. Big Frank will hit it over the pine trees beyond the left centerfield fence." As coaches, we've got to talk about what a player *can* do, not what he can't or might do.

As soon as I returned to the dugout, my right hander delivered a very good fastball right under Thomas's hands. He swung and popped it up on the infield. The entire dugout breathed a sigh of relief, and Steve Culkar came off the mound with a confident smile. I expected an out, Steve expected an out, and he perfectly executed the pitch.

I'm not naïve enough to believe that it always works out that way—but with encouragement, confidence, and execution, the chances are very good that positive results will be accomplished.

Bottom line, as coaches, we should be on the lookout for players who are working hard to improve their weaknesses. When you see progress, it's your job to speak up and clearly let that player know that their hard work is paying off.

Be one of the people in your players' lives who they will talk about for years to come. Be the influence they look back on and say, "Coach believed in me. I would not be doing what I'm doing today if coach had not encouraged me."

Encouragement at the proper time can change the outcome of a game. More importantly, it can change a life.

Grace to Grow

This is not about being perfect or being an expert today. It's about a commitment to grow. Did I blow it during a game? Did I lose my temper with a player or an umpire? The answer is yes—more times than I care to remember. We are all human. But we build our future when we learn from our mistakes and grow as a coach.

Growth doesn't only come from mistakes. Be proactive. As a young college coach, I began conducting summer baseball camps and speaking at civic clubs. Each time I forced myself into these new situations, I became more comfortable as a communicator. The camps helped me become a better instructor. Each speaking engagement helped me become a better presenter. Both helped me lead better team meetings and communicate clearly with players and staff. Eventually, I found my own rhythm, voice, and coaching style.

Investing in yourself as a communicator will only grow your program, your team, and your success. Attend coaching clinics. Read a communication and leadership book during the off-season. Follow coaches who break down fundamentals and progressions well. Put yourself in positions to practice. And give yourself the grace and space to grow over time.

One of the most important roles of a coach is to unleash the inner motivation each player has within. There are goals, dreams, and desires within each athlete you coach. If you connect, if you communicate effectively, you will bring the best out of each player. Not only will your team have a better chance at performing well, but you'll be setting the foundation to create a winning culture.

Remember this: Whoever sows sparingly will also reap sparingly, and whoever sows generously will also reap generously.
—2 Corinthians 9:6 NIV

- 8 -

Winning Culture

*When team members connect and build trust
and strong relationships they don't just work
with each other, they work for each other.*
—*Jon Gordon*

GREATNESS IS A byproduct of risk-taking. In baseball, it's taking an extra base, laying out for a line-drive, taking a hard-hit groundball off the chest, and perhaps throwing a 3-2 breaking ball. Teaching players to take bold, calculated risks starts with building trust—trust in their coach, trust in their teammates, and trust in themselves. When you combine talent and a team-first culture, winning follows.

Back in the '90s, I was working to recruit the top left-hander in the state. Scott Downs was a confident, some would say cocky, pitcher who had a reputation as a great competitor with outstanding command of his fastball and curve. His coach, Bill Miller, was a legend at Pleasure Ridge Park High School (PRP) and throughout the baseball community in the state of Kentucky. I knew I wasn't the only one hoping to recruit from his team.

On this particular day, I was scheduled to do a home visit with Scott and his family. It was about a two-hour drive from UK out to Louisville's south side—enough time to think through how I was going to roll out my recruiting offer as well as the weekend's lineup. Coaches are always balancing executing today while setting up tomorrow. I rolled into town a little early and decided to stop by practice to say hello to Coach Miller.

As I watched PRP wrap up their practice, I noticed the players did an excellent job of raking the field and putting all of the equipment away, not surprising considering Coach Miller's reputation. Soon, almost all the players had left the field with only a couple of assistant coaches left.

I asked one of the assistants, "Coach, where is Scott?" I hoped he hadn't forgotten me! The assistant coach said to me, "Coach, Scott's job after practice today is to clean the restrooms. He should be out soon." I remember thinking, *Wow, the best player in the state is cleaning the restroom after practice!* I wanted Scott to play for Kentucky more than ever.

Coach Miller created a team-first winning culture. Sure, he had great players—Scott was the state's most recruited player that year—but more importantly, they were all in for their team.

PRP went on to win the state tournament that year, and we were fortunate enough to sign Scott Downs with Kentucky. He became the best lefty in the SEC in that era and later pitched 14 years in Major League Baseball. Talent alone isn't always enough. When talent buys into a team-first culture, everyone accomplishes more.

Keys to Culture

A team's culture is the culmination of the habits, behaviors, and ways they function. It's the result of the values they exude and the systems they believe in. We know what a culture feels like—good or bad—but identifying what gets us there isn't quite so straightforward. Culture can't be measured in runs or strikes. There are no stats for measuring teamwork. Yet I believe it's just as important, maybe more so.

Winning culture grows from four things: leadership, defining expectations, setting standards, and commitment to team. Let's take a closer look at each one of them.

1. Leadership

A winning culture starts at the top. Period. A team will only reach a standard as high as the coach has set for himself. The coaches will only be able to build trust with the players to the extent they have built it within the staff. It starts at the head but reaches down to the assistants, trainers, equipment managers, and everyone else connected to the program. A priority for the staff should be building team values with each other and within each player.

Coaching begins with building trust. This starts with communication, which we've already covered. I can't emphasize enough how foundational this area is. You won't ever be perfect, but you can be intentional.

Trust is a two-way street: you want your staff and players to trust you, and you need to be able to trust them. When the bases are loaded (or in any crucial game situation), everything is a mental game. Teams that trust each other stay focused, drawing from a depth of confidence. Together, they can win games against teams with more talent.

While trust starts with communication, it thrives on dignity and respect. How you treat one another matters. This isn't permission to demand submission. True loyalty and respect don't come out of fear—they grow from confidence and trust.

> **TRUE LOYALTY AND RESPECT DON'T COME OUT OF FEAR— THEY GROW FROM CONFIDENCE AND TRUST.**

The players in your care are real people, not pawns on a chessboard. They're younger, still growing and maturing. And they are someone's precious child. Each player is God's unique creation, created in His image. They may look like tough, strong athletes, but everyone has a weak spot. You don't know what might be fragile or even broken on the inside. I've had players step onto the field thriving, while others are doing the best they can to survive complicated home lives, including poverty, abuse, and physical setbacks from accidents or injuries.

Coach, it's your responsibility to treat them with dignity and respect. Demand excellence from them but extend grace when they fail. Push, prod, be intense, but don't break them. Coach them, don't crush their spirits.

> VALUES ARE CAUGHT MORE THAN THEY ARE TAUGHT. YOU CAN SAY THE WORDS ALL YOU WANT, BUT HOW YOU LIVE OUT THE STANDARDS IS WHAT WILL BE FOLLOWED.

Values are caught more than they are taught. You can say the words all you want, but how you live out the standards is what will be followed. You cannot promote a winning culture among your team without developing the right culture within your coaching staff. If players see coaches treating each other (and others) with dignity and respect, it will become contagious. Model the attitudes and behavior you expect from others.

In his first year as head baseball coach at the University of Kentucky, Nick Mingione led the Wildcats into the playoffs. A bid to the super regionals was at stake. I may have been retired from coaching the team, but I certainly wasn't done supporting them. Kentucky was hosting the finals of their NCAA Regional Tournament with a stadium full of excited and energetic fans—the environment was electric! Toward the beginning of a dramatic championship game, a powerful thunderstorm halted play. People scattered and left the stadium, but they didn't go home. They wanted to see the Wildcats win and advance to the Super Regional.

I found shelter within the stadium and when the rain and lightning had subsided, I watched a tremendous example of servant leadership unfold. Kentucky's athletic director, Mitch Barnhart, found a towel and began wiping down the seats for the fans who were re-entering the stadium.

Once Mitch began wiping down the seats, members of his staff began helping. Then random fans began to help, as well, finding anything they could to dry seats for each other.

That is servant leadership. Mitch didn't have to dry seats that day. I'm certain it wasn't in his job description. Many prideful leaders do not consider leading by serving for fear that others may lose respect for them, or they simply think, "I pay others to do that." Did any of the thousands who saw Mitch lead in this way lose respect for him? Quite the contrary; the vast majority gained respect for him. That weekend the crowd helped cheer their team on to the Super Regional.

Mitch Barnhart has created a winning culture in his department on campus—not with words, but by example. Humility is perhaps the most underrated component in constructing a winning culture.

2. Defining Expectations

Another important aspect of a winning culture is defining expectations—both for the individuals and the team.

Recently, I heard former Alabama football coach Nick Saban say, "There is no 'I' in team, but there is an 'I' in win."

We work as a team, but each individual has to do their part. Everyone on the team should know what is expected from him and then take responsibility to pursue the best version of himself. The individual player's pursuit of excellence combined with a team-first mentality is the formula for success.

After the coach defines what is expected from each player, the responsibility now lies with the coaching staff to help each player reach their potential. Coach them up!

The players must understand and be willing to embrace the pursuit of self-discipline. This is a hard concept to teach and it's even harder for a player to conquer.

Self-discipline is knowing what you're supposed to do and then making yourself do it, even when it might be difficult or inconvenient. It's also about knowing what you shouldn't do and then not doing it, even though you really want to do it.

The decisions we make each day add up to hundreds each week and thousands each month. Most of these decisions are out of the coach's reach—you can guide, instruct, suggest, and offer advice but action is up to the individual. Too often we give up and focus only on skills we can measure. Don't.

If we're honest, living out the virtue of self-discipline is hard for coaches. Our instant gratification culture isn't helping any of us. Yet, instead of shying away from the challenge, we should be even more intentional to develop skills and create positive habits. It's the only proven path to achievement in any area of life and a foundation to possessing good character.

We will not always get it right. We all have weak moments. Keeping these weak moments to a minimum is paramount in building a strong winning culture. Coaches must do their best and then trust athletes to follow through. How well coaches teach self-discipline is huge in building a winning culture.

3. Setting Standards

Standards shouldn't be determined by who you are playing. You can play hard and lose. You can play poorly and win. Great preparation leads to competing at a high level, no matter the opponent. What the team puts into developing their skills, conditioning, and effort in practice is what they'll get out come game time.

> YOU CAN PLAY HARD AND LOSE. YOU CAN PLAY POORLY AND WIN. GREAT PREPARATION LEADS TO COMPETING AT A HIGH LEVEL, NO MATTER THE OPPONENT.

If you constantly need to remind players to spend extra time in the batting cage or in the weight room, there's a problem. If they can't give a great effort during baserunning drills and conditioning, you need to work more on team culture. The baseball season can be a grind if athletes aren't in shape. Players need to know why conditioning is vital:

- Being able to sustain great effort from the first pitch to the last comes down to desire and conditioning.

- A player can't stay focused mentally unless he's in peak physical condition.

This extra work, and doing it with excellence, will help defeat opposing teams with more talent. It also gives teams an edge during double-headers and in tournaments. The confidence earned in conditioning and extra cage work may very well be the difference maker at the end of the schedule when the success of the season is on the line.

Each player needs to know that the field, the bullpens, and the batting cages are places of teaching and learning. They are places for fun, but not for goofing off. They are also places where athletes should feel safe. A place they should want to go. A place where they will hear the truth, work hard, pursue excellence, and be encouraged by both coaches and teammates.

Set the standard. Communicate your expectations. And hold players accountable. You can do this without shaming or embarrassing players. Remember, the respect you model is the respect you'll get. But don't be afraid to pull a player aside for a one-on-one. And if they won't put it the effort, a little view from the bench may do them good. Talent is important, but the higher they climb the more competitive baseball will be, and the more important their standards of excellence will be in helping them stand out and get ahead.

4. Commitment to Team

At the end of the day, baseball is a team sport. A pitcher can't win without the outfield, the infield, or the catcher. A phenomenal hitter can't drive in runs without other teammates getting on base. Players need to put in individual effort, but they also must be committed to the team.

Commitment in practice, strength and conditioning, academics, and to the team standards is paramount to a winning culture. If a player or group of players aren't buying in, it can bring the entire team down.

Coaches, it's your responsibility to clearly communicate your vision and philosophy. Keep working on these skills. Keep working on building rapport and trust. This doesn't mean every player is going to like it. They may not like the strategy you chose ("wasting" an at bat with a sacrifice, demanding a competitive two strike hitting approach, etc.). Listen to their concerns—especially if they come to you respectfully, in private and one-on-one. In fact, your players should all know that they can come to you and ask questions. It doesn't mean you have to change your plan, but you can give them the opportunity to be heard.

That said, you shouldn't tolerate negativity. If a player or a group of players don't buy in, their playing time should be limited until they are willing to be a respectful team player.

In a winning culture, players also hold each other accountable for the commitment needed to win. Coaches can't possibly be everywhere at all times. Players holding each other accountable, in the right way, will go a long way.

Every Team Needs Its Own Story

Each year a team will develop its own, unique personality. It's easy for a coach to get caught up into comparing last year's team with this year's group. Just like the individual players on your team, each team has its own unique strengths and weaknesses. The core values should remain the same year after year, but each year a team will leave its own personal legacy in the program. Great coaches adapt and adjust depending on the dynamics of the team.

If a coach helps each player find and define his own purpose, it's a win. Also, if a coach helps each team find and define its own identity, the players will embrace that unique identity, and the season will be more fun.

Baseball is a game. Teams train, compete, and have fun. Baseball is fun, right? Coaches hold the key to the beautiful balance of high-level competition and the enjoyment players have while competing.

Take Them off the Field

Sometimes the best way to build team culture is to take the team off the field. Get them out of their everyday environment, out of their comfort zone, and help them share an experience.

Many of the top college programs and even some of the Major League teams provide opportunities for athletes to serve on campus and in the community. When coaches step up first, players will serve well.

I've taken hundreds of high school and college athletes to the Dominican Republic to not only experience some great baseball, but also to provide opportunities to serve the less fortunate. The players have never disappointed me. Given the chance, players will usually exceed all expectations.

Teaching athletes the value of serving is lifechanging. If you have players on your team who feel entitled, or if they have been sheltered from the poverty and desperation in a third world country (or even just a few miles from their home), get them out of their comfort zone and watch their hearts change. It shouldn't be just a one-time thing, but something that is a part of your program. Whether it's through the organization I work with, SCORE International, or another non-profit, give your players an opportunity to grow through serving. The purpose of serving is to help people who are hurting. I've always found that the ones who serve are blessed more than the ones who are being served.

If you coach youth teams, travel teams, or high school teams, parents are usually stretched. Communicate early. Give them dates and share your why. And keep it simple. They often appreciate the opportunity and are more supportive when it's not a last-minute surprise.

> **NOT ONLY WILL YOU TEACH YOUR TEAM TO CARE FOR THEIR GREATER COMMUNITY, BUT YOU'LL ALSO SEE THEM BUILD BONDS WITH EACH OTHER BY WORKING OFF THE FIELD.**

With these service opportunities, whether in your area, another state, or overseas, whatever is invested will be returned in abundance. Not only will you teach your team to care for their greater community, but you'll also see them build bonds with each other by working off the field.

Develop Servant Leadership

As I mentioned above, coaches can't be everywhere and handle everything. A huge component of creating a winning culture is the opportunity to develop servant leaders within the team. Skills and talent are important recruiting factors, but so are attitude and work ethic. Look for them. Encourage them. And most importantly, model them.

There are many coaches, managers, statesmen, and military leaders to learn from when it comes to leadership styles. Not many totally model servant leadership. Most of my coaches when I was a player were knowledgeable and effective, but they sought little feedback and were of the opinion, "Either do it my way or sit on the bench."

This leader is often so focused on outcomes and perception that they lead by controlling. They see discipline as punishment, often doing more harm than good. Leadership pioneer Ken Blanchard describes them as self-serving leaders who always feel they are in a rat race, "As Lily Tomlin once said, 'The problem with a rat race is that even if you win, you're still a rat.'" On the other hand, the other-oriented servant leaders work side-by-side to help bring out the best in their people. This leader crafts the vision and goals and then helps others live it out.

Servant leadership, from a coaching perspective, is simply coming to the realization that our job as a coach is to teach, encourage, direct, and serve players. The better we serve, the more rewarding the success.

Serving players doesn't mean that you give them the reigns or minimize your position as the coach. It means that you model what it means to enjoy the success of others as much as your own success. It also means adding value to others. It's like giving someone a gift and being more excited about it than the recipient.

Servant leaders are far more likely to have loyal players. Players who play for servant leaders have the unique opportunity to see the coach's heart. Players who play for servant leaders will do anything for the coach because they know the coach will do anything for them.

> SERVING PLAYERS DOESN'T MEAN THAT YOU GIVE THEM THE REIGNS OR MINIMIZE YOUR POSITION AS THE COACH. IT MEANS THAT YOU MODEL WHAT IT MEANS TO ENJOY THE SUCCESS OF OTHERS AS MUCH AS YOUR OWN SUCCESS.

You can still be yourself and be a servant leader. Some coaches have a negative view of servant leadership. They see it as soft or non-competitive. Nothing is further from the truth. A coach who buys in to servant leadership must still provide direction and share a compelling vision. They must have high standards for themselves and the team. They must also be organized, knowledgeable, and decisive. The coach sets the tone for excellence.

Through servant leadership you are living out the concept that we are building something together. Instead of lording over players you are actually leading them. You are helping players to do what they do well even better. If you only love baseball, this is a tough concept. If you love the players who play baseball, it's a natural outflow.

Success is wonderful, of course, but success isn't just about winning. It's also about learning how to build positive memories for your players. It's about developing a winning, competitive mindset in each individual. And it's about teaching players how to put team success ahead of individual accomplishments—a skill that will help them build a better world wherever life takes them.

We can choose to use our passion, our skills, and our gifts to help others grow. When you lead with trust and respect, clearly defined expectations, and model self-discipline, high-standards, and commitment to the team, you'll create a winning culture. With that, you can take your team from good to great.

The greatest among you should be like the youngest, and the one who rules like the one who serves.
—Luke 22:26

PART 3:
THIRD BASE

Champion Execution

- 9 -

Decision Making
SCIENCE IS ORGANIZED KNOWLEDGE.

Wisdom is organized life.
—Immanuel Kant

JOE BLANTON NEVER wanted to be taken out of a game. In his junior year at Kentucky, he was the most dominant pitcher in the SEC. Late in the season that year, on a very warm day in a crucial game against Florida, he was dominating like he never had before. There must have been twenty-five professional scouts in the stands since Big Joe was projected to go in the first round of the draft.

It was late in the game and Joe's pitch count was getting high. We had a two-run lead, but he had allowed a couple of baserunners. My gut and Joe's pitch count were telling me that I needed to take him out of the game. My mind was racing. Why bring in someone from the bullpen when Blanton had the best stuff not only on my roster but in the entire league?

I had only a few seconds to decide whether to take a mound visit and then motion for the right-hander to trot in from the bullpen. On my trip to the mound, Joe was giving me that look that said, "This is one of the biggest games of my life. Don't even think about taking the ball out of my hand."

Out of the hundreds of pitchers I had coached, Blanton was the toughest of all when it came to taking him out of the game. He was extremely competitive. Even though he had a great smile and was soft spoken, he would become a fierce warrior on the mound and could stare hitters down in a way that could make a Viking tremble. Before making it all the way to the mound, Joe said with clinched jaws, "Coach, I am not coming out of this game."

The 6'3" 240 lb. broad-shouldered righthander was determined to get the final outs of the game and he was staring me down as if I was the opposing hitter. He convinced me that he was still strong, and our catcher agreed that his "stuff" was still good. I had just a couple of seconds to make up my mind since the home plate umpire had now joined us on the mound. "Okay Joe, you are the right man for the job," I said.

As soon as I made it back to the dugout, I turned to watch the next pitch. It was a fastball out over the plate. The Florida hitter squared it up perfectly and it sailed deep over the right field fence. The decision was made. It was the wrong decision. Florida now had the lead. They held the lead in the bottom of the ninth and we lost the game.

Even though Joe's pitch count was past his normal limit for effectiveness, and even though my gut had told me to go to the bullpen for a fresh arm, I listened to an ultra-competitive, talented 21-year-old pitcher. It could have worked out differently. Joe could have gotten the out. Or I could have gone to the bullpen and the fresh arm could have either gotten the out or given up the home run. Who knows? But I had to live with my decision.

Whether it's the players in the dugout, the athletic director, the fans, or the parents, someone is watching and counting on your decisions. As coaches, we are often the harshest critic of our own decisions. Coaches make hundreds of decisions every day—many of them in a split second during the course of a game. How do we determine if we're making the best possible choices and moving things in the right direction?

There's no guaranteed formula, but just like a good off-season training program paves the way for a better season, you've got to build the skill of decision making by doing your prep work, seeking wisdom, and putting it into practice.

Preparation

There is more knowledge available to coaches today than ever before. It can make your head spin! We can't absorb it all—nor should we. But growing in our skills and understanding of the game, mastering coaching techniques, learning sport psychology and mental toughness, and developing leadership skills should be a core value.

- Read a couple of dynamic books on the art of leadership each year.
- Listen to relevant podcasts.
- Attend coaching clinics in the off-season.
- Network and develop an inner circle of trusted coaches from other programs that you can brainstorm and share ideas with.

Just as you expect your players to put in their time training, grow yourself as a coach.

Growing in your knowledge of the game is a start. But skills and strategy alone are not enough to prepare you for all the decisions you're going to make.

Know Your Numbers

Whether we like it or not, sabermetrics has revolutionized the game. Gathering statistical data on each player and analyzing performance is a great tool for getting a clear and objective look at where you are and what needs to happen—take advantage of the math and science to inform your decision making.

The term *sabermetrics* wasn't used prior to the 21st century, but teams utilized performance stats with spray charts, radar guns, scouting reports, and multiple other charts updated on clip boards in the dugout. These charts, pitch tendencies, defensive positioning, and pitching/hitting matchups were utilized in real time during games. With today's technology, this same data is more accurate with less human error.

Even if you are an old school coach and resist technology in your dugout, most players you'll coach have grown up using the latest technology and analysis. Even many high school teams are using high-resolution cameras and radar equipment to track velocity from the mound, off the bat, and also from the arms of position players. It's important for coaches to keep up with the terminology for the purpose of good communication and, when possible, use sabermetrics so that your program will not be at a disadvantage.

I must have watched between 45–50 college baseball games in person or on television this past spring. Besides serving as color analyst for home games on the UK Sports Network Radio, I make it to Omaha each spring to represent the ABCA and SCORE International at the College World Series. Watching from up in the radio booth gives me a good view on the defensive shifts that are used frequently in this modern era of baseball.

As much as hitters and many fans hate seeing the shift, coaches are using the data they have to make good decisions on adjusting the infield. Sure, there were a few occasions when the hitter bunted to the weak side or purposely beat the shift by going the other way, but in the end, the numbers don't lie. The shift works against pull happy hitters. If hitters don't make the adjustment, the defense will win the chess match.

So, what does it look like to incorporate the data well? I always appreciate looking at how some of the greatest Major League coaches and managers approach analytics. Their examples might surprise you.

In an interview for "Baseball Stories" with Jayson Stark, former Major League manager Buck Showalter shared his secret to success. "The analytics and the statistics are great," Showalter noted. "I use them. We were using them back in 1985 in the Florida State League. My wife was keeping a chart on all our pitchers. The key is working together and using all your resources—observations on the field, your understanding of your players, and the numbers. But I want that to verify what my gut tells me ..."

No matter what era you play or coach, there will always be newer technology, new tools, new ways to look at the stats. The key isn't having the latest camera, tracker, or analytics app—it's about being intentional in how you apply it.

Showalter takes that next step when he asks his team, "Tell me what this tells us, and then tell me what it doesn't tell us ... Players can't feel like you're robotically evaluating them with a piece of paper." He was concerned with knowing his players. "They're a human being, and sometimes that's the separator in this game."

Terry Francona, another Major League manager, lead with the same principal and shared with Jayson Stark: "When I was back with the Phillies in the late 90s, we weren't very good. I didn't have a computer. I did everything by hand. But I think there were things I believed in that I tried to do. I didn't even know that it was called analytics."

Francona went onto other organizations that were implementing new metrics. By the time he was with Cleveland, the analytics team built the reports to focus on what he valued so he could understand it. "If you don't understand it, it doesn't help anybody. It might look good, but it doesn't help."

At the same time, Francona never stopped just because it was new or different. "The stuff I don't understand, I always check it out because I love when somebody makes me think about something. I may not agree with it, but if they can make me think about it, I really enjoy that."

In order for that to happen, Francona had to create a culture where guys knew they could bring new strategies and ideas to the table. "I think they know that ... the kids bring down stuff all the time and I say, 'Okay, explain this to me because I want to understand,' and I think it's made us better."

Know Your Players

Analytics are incredibly useful for a coach, but numbers can't evaluate a player's confidence, energy, or effort. For that, you've got to know your players.

You might look at last week's stats and notice your six-hole hitter had really poor numbers. You know he's been struggling at the plate, but he's solid defensively and has been in the lineup for the first 15 games. You've got to decide if it's time to change it up or coach him up.

The series stats aren't going to tell you if he's getting overconfident or putting too much pressure on himself. His batting average won't tell you if he's stressed about keeping up with classes or dealing with a difficult situation at home. The numbers will help you identify an issue objectively, but in order to figure out what to do about it, you have to know your player.

> **THE NUMBERS WILL HELP YOU IDENTIFY AN ISSUE OBJECTIVELY, BUT IN ORDER TO FIGURE OUT WHAT TO DO ABOUT IT, YOU HAVE TO KNOW YOUR PLAYER.**

If he's young, could more time and experience to build his mental toughness? Or if he's a perfectionist trying too hard, does he need to step back and watch other players?

What motivates this player? The fear of losing his position, or a few encouraging words to take the pressure off?

If you and your coaching staff are building rapport and communicating with your players, you're going to know the answer. And you're going to make a better decision because of it.

Too often, coaches hold back because of fear of change. It may be time to give this player a break and inject new energy in the lineup with a player who's been waiting for an opportunity to prove himself. The only way you'll know that you aren't giving up on your six-hole hitter is if you know the numbers and know your players—then you'll be able to trust your gut.

Don't Let Emotions Get in the Way

What you value will impact the decisions you make. If you value people over numbers, you will lean toward following your gut feeling. If you are a person who believes that numbers never lie, you'll tend to trust the analytics over feelings. Great leaders use both their gut feelings and the numbers.

One season, sometime midway through my coaching career at Kentucky, we were playing at home. It was a beautiful, sunny day. I became aware of the young new umpire strutting behind home plate. My mind began to wonder how this guy could be experienced enough to handle a Division I game. (He may have thought the same thing about me, of course.)

There were a couple of questionable calls, in my opinion. If we aren't careful and emotions get involved, we can start to feel like we have to stand up for our team or a particular player who found himself on the wrong end of a questionable call. And on this particular day, my overcharged "protection" got me tossed from the game.

Later that season, the same young umpire was assigned to a crucial SEC series. When I saw him walk in the gate with the other umpires, I had a sense of doom. Just seeing this guy clouded my judgement the entire day.

I watched his every move. I just knew he was going to blow another call. With every inning I waited for him to mess up, I became a lesser version of my best self. Instead of focusing on managing my team, I was spending a whole lot of energy attempting to manage an umpire.

My gut feeling was based one hundred percent on my emotions and completely ignoring the analytics. He was one of the top-rated umpires in the league. His numbers were very good. If I had trusted his numbers and ability more, it would have helped me concentrate more on my players and the things I could control.

In spite of our best intentions to stick to the facts, we are still human. Previous experience and personal bias can still creep into our decision making and skew the information. We can't be all in the numbers or all in our gut. We need them both.

Seek Wisdom

Trusting yourself in the decision-making process is huge. We can show confidence in the dugout, but that doesn't mean you aren't carrying a load of stress inside. Knowledge is important—you've got to have the facts and know the fundamentals. If you don't, take the time to pursue them. But all the knowledge in the world can't make us wise.

While many coaches look for the latest techniques, drills, or catchy phrases to secure the competitive edge, the most successful coaches see themselves primarily as leaders—responsible for leading and guiding people— and seek wisdom. Coaches like John Wooden, Tony Dungy, John Scolinos, Jerry Kendall, and Mark Johnson have set themselves apart, coaching and leading on a different plane. One common denominator stands out— they all sought wisdom.

Eighteenth century German philosopher Immanuel Kant once said, "Science is organized knowledge. Wisdom is organized life." Wisdom is crucial in timing, communication, and most definitely decision making. You cannot lead well without it.

So how do we gain wisdom? Albert Einstein said, "Wisdom is not a product of schooling but of the life-long attempt to acquire it." While I agree you can't learn wisdom in a textbook, must we wait a lifetime to acquire it? Sure, experience is a key factor in building wisdom, but I don't believe it's the only way we gain it.

We have access to wisdom now, in the present, through faith. *"If any of you lacks wisdom, you should ask God, who gives generously to all without finding fault, and it will be given to you"* (James 1:5).

This is one of my go-to Bible verses and an incredible promise. Written to encourage the Jewish Christians who had been scattered abroad to escape persecution, it is full of promise and assurance.

Let's look at some of those promises:

1. **If you need wisdom—and we all need it every day—ask God.** Not only will God give you wisdom, but He also gives generously! As mentioned before, coaches make numerous decisions every day and during each game. Generosity is one God's many amazing attributes. When we ask, He not only gives to us what we need, He gives abundantly. This is a great example given to decision makers. Coaches and leaders should be generous with a listening ear and the knowledge and wisdom they have been granted.

2. **He gives to all without finding fault.** If it depended on being perfect, none of us would be worthy enough to ask God for wisdom. But because of God's great grace, available freely through our faith in him, we are encouraged to ask. There's no list of qualifications or goodness.

It doesn't matter why we need it or where we are. He gives because we ask.

3. **It's a promise we can trust.** *"...ask God ... and it will given to you."* Period.

Asking for wisdom is an intentional practice. Before every important decision or meeting, especially if they might involve conflict, I ask God for wisdom. When I remember to ask, these consequential decisions and meetings may not be easy, but they *always* turn out better than I expected.

At game time, I intentionally took the moment right before play while the National Anthem was playing to pray silently and ask God for wisdom to coach the game. It was the calm before the storm—a time to thank God for the freedom we have in our nation and to ask Him for wisdom as I led the team into competition.

Wisdom is the best tool in a leader's toolbox. It's available to all who believe and ask—but very few people ask.

King Solomon, the wise and rich king of ancient Israel, wrote the following to the future leaders and generations in his time: *"Do not forsake wisdom, and she will protect you; love her and she will watch over you. The beginning of wisdom is this: get wisdom. Though it cost all you have, get understanding"* (Proverbs 4:5–7).

To be the best coach you can be, make sure that asking for wisdom is included in every major decision, meeting, practice, and game. Nothing else matches it.

4 Principals to Practice

Effective decision making starts with knowledge and wisdom, but it also means taking action. Here are four principals I find helpful to keep moving forward.

1. Steer Clear of Procrastination

Procrastination is the enemy of both progress and success. I developed the negative habit of procrastinating while studying for exams in college. To be honest, it's still a problem for me in certain situations. In coaching, it didn't rear its ugly head often because my staff and team depended on me.

Waiting to decide isn't always procrastination. It's necessary, at times, to gather more information or to allow yourself more options before making a final decision. What happens, occasionally, is that we may push a decision into the back of our minds while waiting for more options and then make a hasty decision instead of a well-though-out, planned solution.

Important decisions need to be kept in the front of our minds and at the top of our to-do list. A leader should set a date for the decision to be made. In other words, decide when you will decide.

The weight of unmade decisions can be heavy. A successful coach should never fear making important decisions. Being decisive helps take that weight off you; it gives you more freedom and mobility moving forward.

2. *Coach Yourself*

Coaches are constantly giving advice, offering tips, and sharing life lessons with others. As coaches gain experience, most become good with helping others make decisions. So why not ask yourself, "What advice would I give someone else who needs to make this decision?" Other times, you may need to ask yourself, "What would a great coach do in this situation?"

Some of you may remember the WWJD bracelets that became popular in the '90s. The acronym stands for "What Would Jesus Do?" It became somewhat of a cliché, but the premise is excellent. Jesus is the greatest teacher and has more knowledge and wisdom than anyone else, so don't fear asking yourself that question.

All too often it's our fears and emotions that keep us from confidently stepping forward. Whether it's a fear of failure or feeling protective of a person or idea, our emotions can hold us back. Author and pastor Craig Groeschel has a tactic for overcoming fear paralysis. He takes a step back from the situation and asks himself, "What would my successor do?" Suddenly, the emotion is out of it. If someone new came in, someone with no connection to the history behind a situation, what would they objectively choose? Oftentimes it makes the path forward crystal clear.

3. Delegate

If you're trying to handle everything without help, you're setting yourself up for fatigue or burnout. Leaders are not designed to carry the entire load—

> **LEADERS ARE NOT DESIGNED TO CARRY THE ENTIRE LOAD—THE JOB IS TO DEVELOP OTHER LEADERS.**

the job is to develop other leaders. Your need to control every situation will only pave the way for frustration and failure. So, delegate as much as possible to the people on your team.

This might be assistant coaches. If you're a travel ball coach, it may mean asking parents to step up and coordinate details like water, meals, and collecting everyone's shirt size. It might be players—team captains and other experienced players ought to be stepping up in their skills on the field, but also in their responsibility to lead the team.

Often during my career, one of my assistant coaches would come into my office or approach me on the field and ask, "Coach, here's the situation. What do you want me to do?" Sometimes I would say, "You make the decision. You have my support." This not only takes part of the load off the head coach, but it also tells the assistant coach, "I believe in you."

Will there be mistakes? Sure. We all make a bad call now and then. Mistakes are one of the most significant ways we grow. Instead of berating an assistant (or yourself) about a mistake, take the opportunity to ask, "What would you do differently if you had it to do over?"

If you believe that you are the only one who can make a wise decision, you are either overconfident in your leadership ability or you are hiring the wrong assistants. Delegate often. Give staff members freedom to grow. Extend grace and tolerance. And remember, you are developing leaders. In the long run, a more confident and capable staff will be helping you lead successfully.

Trusting your staff doesn't mean you don't care. It simply means that you trust and believe in the people you have hired to help lead your program. The head coach is still the leader—at the end of the day, you must bear the responsibility. Leading well, means that you are developing leaders while ultimately taking risks and taking the heat. As President Harry Truman often said, "If you can't stand the heat, get out of the kitchen."

4. Avoid "Either-Or"

Decisions often present themselves as a "this or that" choice. Do you want to run this drill or that one? Do you want John or Miguel to be the leadoff hitter this weekend? At face value, it seems like a simple decision: do you want choice A or B? But in fact, this limited choice may actually be limiting the possibility. If we want to lead exceptional teams, we've got to expand the options and think outside the box.

For example, an assistant coach might come to you and ask, "Skipper, should we schedule either two practices each day, or one practice and weight-lifting each day during fall break?" If you get boxed in to "either-or" you are limited. You might just do what you've always done. But what if you opened up the options?

> IF WE WANT TO LEAD EXCEPTIONAL TEAMS, WE'VE GOT TO EXPAND THE OPTIONS AND THINK OUTSIDE THE BOX.

Let's assume you know your players. You know you've recruited a solid lineup of committed athletes. Most of them played all summer long and may have been practicing six days per week since fall practice began. How are they doing? Are they tired? Sore? Spending more time in the training room than the classroom ... and it's not even in season?

If you open up the options, you can look at all the angles. Could you give them part or all of the week off to rest their bodies and enjoy life away from baseball for a few days? Could you take the team off the field and cross train or focus on teambuilding and mental toughness? It might refuel their energy and passion.

When you limit your options to the either-or scenario, you paint yourself in a corner. In most decision-making challenges, there are rarely ever only two options. The bottom line: trust the data, trust your coaching staff, and trust your gut. It doesn't have to be either-or.

Decision making makes or breaks the leader. Put in the preparation, seek wisdom, and allow God to do the rest. We can't control the outcome, but we can control how we handle what we do next.

Trust in the Lord with all your heart and lean not on your own understanding; in all your ways submit to Him, and He will make your paths straight.
—Proverbs 3:5-6

- 10 -

Bouncing Back

With everything that has happened to you, you can feel sorry for yourself or treat what has happened as a gift. Everything is either an opportunity to grow or an obstacle to keep you from growing. You get to choose.
—*Wayne Dyer*

BASEBALL IS THE greatest sport, but bottom line—it's filled with failure.

Pitchers throw a small, hard sphere at high velocity. Hitters are supposed to hit the center of the baseball with a bat that is also rounded. To make it a little more difficult, the ball that is traveling at near 100 mph at the highest levels of the game doesn't travel on a straight path.

A fastball travelling at 90 mph takes .4 seconds to reach home plate after it leaves the pitcher's hand, but a hitter needs a full .25 seconds to see the ball and react. The reaction time is similar to the speed of blinking an eye.

Sometimes the ball sinks, sometimes it appears to rise, sometimes it tails away, and other times it cuts in. It can appear to be a fastball, but then suddenly it slides. At times, the ball seems to be spinning high in the strike zone, but late in its journey it spins down in the zone.

And that's not all. As a hitter stands at the plate ready to swing his bat, there are eight fielders staring him down—each one just waiting to catch whatever he hits and record an out.

No wonder even most of the Major League hitters fail over 70% of the time. Even Ty Cobb, who's held a top spot for the highest career batting average at .366 since the 1920s, failed well over 60% of the time. Playing baseball is hard. Hitting a baseball is very hard.

But baseball isn't just an individual measure of precision and skill. It's a team sport. And there's another type of failure—losing the game.

The baseball schedule contains more games than any other sport. In the Major Leagues, 162 games are played between April and the beginning of October. Minor League teams play between 132–150 games between early April and early September. And NCAA Division 1 Baseball teams play 56 games between the middle of February and the middle of May. All these games add up to a whole lot of pitches, runs, and outs.

Hopefully teams win a lot—but there's also a whole lot of losses. The numbers can take a toll. Coaches who learn how to bounce back will always have the edge on those who allow a loss to carry over to the next game.

Failure is Not Fatal

Talk to any successful coach and they will tell you the same thing—very little is learned during a win. Losses are painful, but they are significant in the learning process.

We have to teach our hitters to shake off a bad at bat, and our pitchers to shake off a poor inning. We need to practice how to transition from the disappointment of a loss to refocus before the next time the umpire says, "Play ball!"

> RESILIENCE REQUIRES PERSEVERANCE AND PROBLEM SOLVING. WHEN WE LEARN TO BOUNCE BACK AS COACHES, WE LEAD OUR TEAM AND STAFF TO BOUNCE BACK WITH US.

Resilience requires perseverance and problem solving. The good news is, when we learn to bounce back as coaches, we lead our team and staff to bounce back with us. Here are a few principals to keep in mind.

It Starts with You

Much of coaching is about facing challenges and solving problems. If you are running from challenges, you will not be effective.

As a young coach, I struggled with recovering after a loss. All my losses were painful, but early in my career I had a hard time turning it around quickly and being ready for the next game. I don't think I could have made it through all those years of coaching had I not learned how to bounce back.

You can't pursue excellence as a coach unless you're willing to meet problems head on with wisdom, toughness, and empathy. And if you want your team to handle the pressure, you've got to make sure you're leading the way.

Plan for Success

Set realistic goals. Every coach would love to be conference champs. Is that realistic with the team and circumstances you have right now? Don't give up on that goal. But you might need to set short-term goals during the season in order to build a team that can take it to that level.

Start with goals that can create more success. Visualize how this season, this lineup, will play out—if you can't see it happen in your mind, it most likely won't happen in real life.

Very few challenges are true surprises. Most of the time if we stop and think it through, we can anticipate the bumps ahead. Say your new starting pitcher is a guy we'll call Joe. He's a righthander and earned the spot this week. You know from the stats that he's got a good fastball, but he's not been throwing well against lefties. Now chances are, Joe is going to meet a few lefties in the lineup. What is this going to look like? Will he give up a hit that allows the go ahead run? Could he allow a home run that changes the momentum of the game? Or worse?

Take time to anticipate the problems and strategize solutions. Your plan to counter the problem might look like any of these options:

A. Making sure the pitching coach is working with him on a change-up so that the left-handed hitters timing is off;

B. Building up his confidence to throw the fastball under the hitter's hands to set up the change he will try to locate down and away; or

C. Planning ahead to have a reliever ready in a crucial situation (preferably a left hander with good stuff!).

Your job is to make sure your players have the skills and the support to meet the challenge. Visualize the roadblocks—as much as possible—think a game ahead, an inning ahead, and a pitch ahead.

Surround Yourself with Winners

Inevitably, we adopt habits and attitudes similar to the people we spend the most time with. If you hang around negative people, you will become more negative. If you spend time with quality, positive people, you will become more positive. Some people hang out with skunks, then wonder why they smell. Don't allow a negative, loser mentality dominate who you are. Choose who you surround yourself with.

Ask for Accountability

Winning attitudes are one thing; holding each other accountable is another. Coaches are usually good at evaluating the attitudes of team members, but like everyone, they need help in self-evaluation. Accountability is not about criticism—it's about helping each other become the best leaders, coaches, husbands, parents, and citizens we can possibly be. Winners get there together.

> ACCOUNTABILITY IS NOT ABOUT CRITICISM—IT'S ABOUT HELPING EACH OTHER BECOME THE BEST LEADERS, COACHES, HUSBANDS, PARENTS, AND CITIZENS WE CAN POSSIBLY BE. WINNERS GET THERE TOGETHER.

There was a time when the SEC only had ten teams. During a part of that era, baseball played the conference schedule without divisions. One of those years, we were heading into the second half of the conference schedule and six of the ten teams were only separated by about 2 ½ games—including us.

Going into a road series against the last place team in the conference, I was confident that if we swept them—or even won two of three—we would move up in the standings and put ourselves in a position to challenge for the regular season title.

Instead, we were rained out of the Saturday doubleheader, had another rain delay on Sunday, and proceeded to lose both games. The long, late bus ride back to Lexington was not pleasant for anyone—partly because I had the disposition of an angry hornet.

We rolled into Lexington at about 4:00 a.m. Monday morning. I remember standing before the team and bellowing, "Some of you have eight o-clock classes this morning and I recommend that you attend. I will personally be checking attendance at random classrooms."

I slept for a couple of hours in my office and woke up grumpier than ever. I couldn't wait to get to practice. It was going to be the most grueling practice of the year. I was going to show my players the price you pay for losing to the last place team in the league!

When I pulled in the parking lot at Shively Sports Center, I noticed our football coach, Bill Curry, pull in next to me. It wasn't uncommon for us to cross paths as we shared the training center with football and track. Coach Curry and I stepped out of our vehicles at the same time. Before he went on to spring practice, he paused, turned to me, and said, "Keith, I saw in the paper this morning where you dropped two over the weekend. I know how badly you needed those wins."

Then he looked at me for a moment and with a serious expression on his face said, "If you go out on the practice field looking like you do now, it's going to be a miserable practice. You look terrible! I suggest you go into the locker room and while you are changing into your practice gear, you also change your attitude. If you go out on the field looking like you do right now, you will have your worst practice of the season. Remember, you have LSU coming in this weekend and they are ranked number one. You can't turn your team around unless you turn yourself around."

Wow! It wasn't what I expected. But it was a wakeup call from a good man—a man whom I respected and held in high esteem. After that challenge, I took myself to the locker room, showered, changed into my practice gear, and then walked out to the field with a different attitude.

Instead of hammering my team with a physically demanding practice and showing them who's boss, I simply said, "Let's get this weekend behind us and have a short, crisp practice. We won't be here very long, but while we're on the field, let's get better and have fun doing it."

The next day, Coach Curry and I pulled into the Shively Sports Center at the same time once again. When he got out of the car, he had a big smile on his face and said, "While I was on the tower yesterday, I was trying to concentrate on our practice, but I kept looking over at the baseball field. It looked like you had a great practice. Lots of energy, guys bouncing around."

I thanked him for challenging me to get out of my doldrums the previous day. We made a pact to hold each other accountable concerning our attitudes. Good friends are truthful with one another, even though it might sting in the moment.

By the way, that next weekend we swept the #1 ranked LSU Tigers and climbed a little higher in the conference standings and the national rankings! Without being held accountable for my actions and challenged to change my attitude, I seriously doubt that we would have won even one game against LSU.

Guard Your Heart

When things don't go as planned—and it happens more often than not—the enemies of discouragement and doubt will be battling for control of your heart and mind. The first things they'll do is steal your confidence and rob you of your energy.

This isn't a surprise to God. He knows that during our time on earth we are going to face challenges. We are going to be in battle; our confidence is going to be under attack. Therefore, we must be prepared.

Proverbs 4:23 says, *"Above all else, guard your heart, for everything you do flows from it."* Challenge and doubt shouldn't catch you off guard. You can choose to protect yourself.

Just how do you do this? First and foremost, arm yourself with truth. A single play, game, or season doesn't define you—remember your true identity and purpose. (If you need to, revisit to Chapter 4.) When you stand on the truth of who God says you are and why you're here, you can face the challenges from a position of strength.

Rest & Reset

We can't give 100% without refueling. If hard work is a core value, then rest must be also. Whether it's taking a break to recharge after the end of a season, or a lighter practice at the end of a long road trip, building in moments for resting and resetting fills us up so we can perform to our potential. No one gets very far on an empty tank. Yes, there are times to dig down deep and find a little more. But there's also value in moments of reset—for you and for your team.

Lead Your Team

I don't know any athlete or sports fan that's not competitive. We want to win. A coach with high standards will never accept just enough to get by. Expect excellence and attention to detail in effort and attitude. This shows up in the little things: how you practice the fundamentals, how you take care of the dugout, how you show up on time and in focus for your team. (That applies to players *and* coaches.)

Expect Excellence; Extend Empathy

The challenge is, you can't simply say these things matter—you've got to follow through with consequences, even if it means a game is lost. If your big hitter is late to practice over and over, bench him. If the pitchers are taking shortcuts in drills, run them. Don't accept an attitude of mediocrity.

None of us are perfect. Sometimes we will be outplayed. Sometimes we have a bad day. There are games when your team will play very well, but still lose. When the results aren't what you want them to be, extend empathy. Empathy says I understand, and I believe if we stay the course and continue to work on improving both skills and mental toughness, we will succeed again another day.

Expect excellence in effort and extend empathy when players give all they've got, but things don't go your way.

Tweak but Don't Change

This doesn't mean we don't have to make changes. Sometimes the most empathetic thing we can do is give a player who's wrapped up in his doubt or stress a break. But don't make drastic changes. Stick to your plan.

Too often we end up playing musical chairs trying to find the perfect lineup. This only confuses players—or worse, causes them to lose confidence in themselves and in you. It's okay to tweak things here or there, but don't make major changes in the middle of the season unless it's absolutely necessary.

Address the Cause

Analyze what went wrong. This comes right back to knowing your numbers and knowing your players. (We talked about this in the last chapter.) Wisdom and empathy will help you discern the root of the problem.

Your solution should look different if it's a failure of attitude or effort versus a weak spot in skills. Leaning into the stats while also knowing your players will give you the confidence to know when to sit someone and when to stick with him.

A hitter may be one for his last 15 at bats, but if he has hit hard line drives for outs eight or ten times, he needs to be encouraged, not benched. Tell him, "I love the way you're swinging the bat. Don't do anything different. Keep squaring it up, the hits will come."

Move Past Emotions

Fans love to see confrontations on the field, especially from a coach. You'll get all kinds of attention when you look like Earl Weaver or Billy Martin. Some say it shows how much you care. Even some of your players will applaud. They often say, "Look how he's standing up for the team!" But as you "stand" for the team, are you representing the program and school in a poor light?

Coaches, be passionate. Exude energy. But for the sake of your athletes, be in control. Be poised. Ice hockey fans love a good brawl, too. But just because it gets attention doesn't mean it has anything to do with winning the game, let alone improving the season.

Be sure you're "there" for your team in stressful and emotional situations. It's really not that difficult to lead when things are going well. It's the losing streaks, the bad calls, and the days when the other team shows you up that elevates the blood pressure and causes us to do and say things we would never say or do off the field. Coaches, remember your players are watching, your family is watching, and your bosses are probably watching. All reasons to "count to ten" and be in control. The worst decisions are made when your emotions are at a boiling point.

I read many biographies. Recently, I've read books about Ulysses S. Grant and Robert E. Lee. Both generals were lauded by their contemporaries for their ability to stay calm during fire. They were both fierce warriors and had an unusual sense of compassion for those they led. They both exuded composure while leading, even when bullets were whizzing past and lives were at stake. When soldiers on either side feared for their lives, they could look to their leaders for both courage and strength of character.

Years ago, I attempted to read *The Purpose Driven Life* by Rick Warren. I was still coaching then. I'm embarrassed to say that I didn't get past the first page on my initial attempt. Why? Because at the bottom of the first page Rick said, "It's not about you." I remember thinking, *Hey, if this book isn't about helping me, then why read it?* I was immediately stunned by the selfishness of my inner thoughts. So, the following month I picked up the book and read it every morning until completion. The book has helped millions discover their purpose in life. It helped me to rediscover mine.

When the going gets tough, take the focus off of yourself and do what you were called to do: coach, instruct, strategize, compete, encourage your players, and LEAD! It's not about you.

Did I ever blow it during a game? Did I ever lose my temper with an umpire or a player? The answer is yes, a few more times than I care to remember. We are all human and make mistakes. But we are better served if we learn from our mistakes and grow as a coach.

There are times we must minimize our ego, our frustration, and even our anger at the umpires and just coach. This means demanding excellence from your players, making some positive moves, and most of all, encouraging and believing in your players.

Don't look for solutions while you are emotional. You'll overreact. Acknowledge the feeling—it's a signal that there's a problem, not the solution. Go for a long run. Get a lift in. Talk to your best friend and vent for five minutes. Then choose to use your emotions to make yourself, and the team, better. Go do something about it. Focus your energy on problem solving.

Talk to Them

I've said it before, and I'll say it again: If you want your players to perform at their best, you've got to communicate. You can't coach if you don't connect.

No one can read your mind. Not your players, not your assistants, and not even your own family. If you're going to make a change, tell them what you're doing, why you're doing it, and what you want them to work on.

You might have a young player struggling, uptight, and in his own head. Your best move might be to sit him out a game so he can watch more seasoned players. There are times when watching others play gives a player the opportunity to see that he's making the game more difficult than it really is. But you've got to tell him what you're doing. Otherwise, he has no idea you're not planning to bench him for the rest of the season.

Each higher level of play that a player (and coach) enters brings a new level of pressure and the need for greater mental strength. How many times as coaches do we find ourselves wondering when the shoe is going to drop and an AD is going to pull the rug out from under us? Your players feel pressure too. And it's not just college players who are worried someone from the transfer portal is going to be brought in for their position. I hear it in high school and travel ball, too.

Younger and younger, the players are feeling squeezed with pressure to get every throw and every swing just right or else get benched—or not even make a team. Our youth aren't meant to carry this much pressure. They need to be coached up and trained to handle the pressure just as much as they need to hit better, run faster, and throw harder.

Baseball is a mental game; there's no doubt about it. There are no perfect players or perfect coaches—we're all a work in progress. The better you are at bouncing back, the greater the potential you hold for you and your players.

> **THERE ARE NO PERFECT PLAYERS OR PERFECT COACHES—WE'RE ALL A WORK IN PROGRESS. THE BETTER YOU ARE AT BOUNCING BACK, THE GREATER THE POTENTIAL YOU HOLD FOR YOU AND YOUR PLAYERS.**

Let perseverance finish its work so that you may be mature and complete, not lacking anything.
—James 1:4

- 11 -

Character Development

Character is doing the right thing when nobody's looking. There are too many people who think that the only thing that's right is to get by, and the only thing that's wrong is to get caught.
—J. C. Watts Jr.

WE HAVE A crisis in character today. I'm not exaggerating. All you have to do is turn on the news to hear another report of moral failings. Whether it's someone in politics, religion, education, or athletics, someone has cheated, lied, stollen, or swindled. Because of this, people don't know who to trust. Some people trust no one.

I was recently listening to a podcast where the host and guest were discussing how cheating has risen among students. They shared how 88% of the students in one survey reported that they cheat on exams. When asked how many times they have cheated, most of them said, "hundreds of times." Challenge Success, a non-profit connected to the Stanford Graduate School of Education, has reported similar statistics. They found multiple studies reporting 80–95% of high school students admit to some form of cheating.

What do we expect when public leaders are cheating? If they don't have to live honestly, why do students? This is not only a crisis, it's an epidemic.

"Children are 25 percent of the population but 100 percent of the future," author and psychologist Thomas Lickona said in his book, *Character Matters*. "If we wish to renew society, we must raise up a generation of children who have strong moral character. And if we wish to do that, we have two responsibilities: first, to model good character in our own lives, and second, to intentionally foster character development in our young." I wholeheartedly agree.

Coaches, we have a front row seat to the future. Besides teachers and parents, there are few adults with more opportunity to impact the next generation. If we want our communities and our country to have a bright future, it starts with us.

> COACHES, WE HAVE A FRONT ROW SEAT TO THE FUTURE. IF WE WANT OUR COMMUNITIES AND OUR COUNTRY TO HAVE A BRIGHT FUTURE, IT STARTS WITH US.

Competing, winning, teaching fundamentals, recruiting, and managing a game are all extremely important to those of us who love to compete. But, if we leave out character development and leadership within our team, we are failing miserably.

Character Is...

Character is the set of qualities that define a person as an individual. These qualities include honesty, integrity, courage, and respect.

Honesty & Integrity

These two qualities shouldn't need a lot of explanation. Honesty is simply telling the truth, and integrity means living the truth even when no one is watching. The challenge is being honest without being brutal. Do you honestly give feedback in a way that's constructive? Or do you just yell out what your players are doing wrong? Be honest. Be constructive. And be sure you're telling them what they can do to fix it. That's coaching. Putting in the effort to do the work is up to the player.

Courage

Courage is taking action in the face of challenge or fear. As coaches, it's up to us to take the lead. If you want your players to step up, face challenges, and own their mistakes, make sure you're modeling it first. Make the hard call and bench your best player if he keeps showing up to practice late, gives a poor effort, or displays a negative attitude, even if it could cost a game. (It might not.

You might be surprised when someone off the bench performs well.)

Respect

As a teenager (and truth be told, even as a young adult) one of the great motivators for me to do the right thing was the desire to not disappoint my parents. Why? Because I knew they loved me and wanted the best for me, and I respected them. I didn't want to let them down. The same can be said about my coaches—I knew they cared, so I gave a great effort (at least most of the time). I didn't want to disappoint them.

Do your athletes know you care? Do they know you believe in them? The fear of disappointing the people we love and respect can be a greater motivator than punishment. That's just one of many reasons we should pour more than knowledge into our players. Demonstrate—with words and actions—that you're there to bring out the best in them and the team. They won't want to disappoint you if they know it's real.

Living It from the Field

My high school coach, Kaye Don VanMeter, was knowledgeable and was good at teaching skills and leading young men, but his number one attribute was his strength of character.

Coach VanMeter didn't make speeches or talk about character. In fact, he was very quiet and, for the most part, very seldom ever raised his voice. But when he did speak, everyone listened. His steadfastness and consistency were attributes that made an impact on me as a young player. In three years of playing for him, coach was angry with me only one time—and I will never forget it.

We were playing against Caverna High School and the Doyle twins. Bryan and Blake played second and shortstop and also pitched. They were only sophomores, but every player and coach in the state knew about them. The brothers were an incredible middle infield combination, and one of them (I believe it was Blake) could pitch both righthanded and lefthanded. Yogi Berra would have called him "amphibious." Both followed their older brother Denny's footsteps and eventually played Major League Baseball.

Needless to say, it was a big game for us. As a pitcher, I wanted to show the Doyle twins who was boss. You can't say I'm not competitive.

I was at bat mid-way through the game when I drew a walk. As I arrived at first base, I signaled for the equipment manager to bring my pitching jacket. In those days, it was popular for pitchers to wear their pitching jacket between innings and even on the bases. I had watched Tom Seaver and Nolan Ryan do this on television. It was cool. So, I slipped on my jacket and waited for the next play.

There was one out. The next hitter hit a routine groundball right to Brian Doyle at shortstop. With my pitching jacket on I morphed into big league mode and sort of peeled off to the outfield side of second base without sliding or trying to break up the double play. In my mind, it was an automatic double play with the Doyle twins playing in the middle. I wasn't going to slide in my jacket for that.

With the double play turned and the third out recorded, I motioned for the manager to bring my glove and take my jacket back to the dugout. When I looked up, Coach VanMeter was bringing my glove out to the mound.

That's really cool, I thought, *Coach is bringing my glove out. He must be wanting to give me a scouting report on the inning's leadoff hitter.*

Let's just say, that was not his intention! When Coach VanMeter handed my glove to me, I noticed that his face was very red. He proceeded in a tone I had never heard him use before.

"Keith, if you ever fail to run full speed on the bases and not slide to break up a double play, you will be sitting with me in the dugout for a very long time!"

Whew, he was serious! I will never forget that one way conversation. As a matter of fact, even at my advanced age, if I was at first base with less than two outs and someone hit a ground ball, I would be running full speed and I would do everything in my power to break up the double play!

Coach VanMeter taught me two things that day. First, if coaches are always loud, always talking, always yelling and screaming, players become desensitized and eventually pay little attention. If you choose when to instruct or teach a character lesson, players will listen well and will take the instruction with them through life.

Second, he taught me how to play the game the right way—not for myself, but for the team and program. He taught me that I was representing the school, the program, and my family. Everyone was counting on my effort on every play. Not only did Coach VanMeter teach me to be a better ball player, but he also helped me grow my character.

Progress vs Perfection

If we want to build the character of those we coach, we must build our own first. This is a long-term process ... a life-time endeavor. The word "building" sounds like work. It is. But the compensation is self-esteem and respect from those we coach and from our contemporaries.

> **WE DON'T IMPROVE OUR CHARACTER BY MAKING DRASTIC CHANGES OVERNIGHT, WE GROW BY MAKING SMALL CHANGES EVERY DAY THROUGHOUT OUR LIFETIME.**

We don't improve our character by making drastic changes overnight, we grow by making small changes every day throughout our lifetime. Very much like we want our athletes to form good habits on the field and in the classroom, to develop our own character, we must work at it every day.

When I think of men of great character, I don't visualize perfect men. I see men who wanted to do the right thing and made a habit of doing it. As Paul said in Romans 3:23, "For all have sinned and fall short of the glory of God." Even great men and women in history were fallible.

Focus on the Positive

People enjoy pointing their finger at others' mistakes. Somehow, it makes some people feel better about their own shortcomings if they can bring out the faults of noble people.

I once had a history professor who seemed to delight in sharing the faults of men such as Lincoln, Washington, Franklin, and Jefferson. At the beginning it was interesting, and even entertaining; but a few weeks into the course, his methods exposed his own character flaws, and the class became depressing.

What if we spent more time and energy focused on the positive? What if we emphasized the courage and dignity of those who take a stand to make our world a better place—not because they're perfect, but because it's the progress that makes a difference.

In the baseball world, some people can't talk about Mickey Mantle unless they chide him for his drinking problem. The same with Babe Ruth. Pete Rose is the all-time hits leader in Major League Baseball but mention his name and someone will point out his gambling addiction or his association with unsavory characters. Yet, even with their well-documented faults, each of these guys were not only phenomenal players, but they also had positive character traits that are seldom mentioned.

Mantle never, to my knowledge, showed a pitcher up after hitting a mammoth home run. Ruth had a big heart. He visited children in hospitals and helped teammates out of financial jams. Rose taught hundreds of thousands of kids that it's cool to hustle, running out every groundball and playing with passion and energy.

We should never condone the negative behavior of our sports heroes or anyone else, but it is wise to put our own house in order before tearing others down. Constantly bringing up people's character flaws can come across as self-righteous and rarely benefits others.

Inspire Second Chances

When we highlight the positive, we bring the good to the light. We also inspire second chances—for ourselves and the players we work with. No one should be defined only by their mistakes. When we tell the stories of overcomers and the good that can come after mistakes, we make room for people to grow and change.

Bottom line, talking about the positive character traits in any individual is uplifting and beneficial. How often do you speak up about the positive character on your team? It's not enough to say character matters—you've got to recognize it when it shows up: in the lineup, in your awards, in any other privilege offered on your team. If character counts, you have to show it more than you say it.

Stay Humble

Humility is more attractive than over the top swagger in both playing and coaching, in my opinion. Confidence is a must for both players and coaches, but too much showboating is a turnoff. I've always considered boasting and arrogance to be character flaws.

> **IT'S NOT ENOUGH TO SAY CHARACTER MATTERS—YOU'VE GOT TO RECOGNIZE IT WHEN IT SHOWS UP.**

In Jesus's day, some religious leaders, the Pharisees, were steeped in tradition and law and were considered all together righteous. Tax collectors were considered the ultimate sinners. They collected taxes from their fellow Jews and kept a portion of the collections for themselves. They were hated by the Jews and trusted by no one. Jesus shocked both His followers and the Pharisees when He told the following parable:

> *"Two men went up to the temple to pray, one a Pharisee and the other a tax collector. The Pharisee stood by himself and prayed: 'God, I thank you that I am not like other*

people—robbers, evildoers, adulterers—or even like this tax collector. I fast twice a week and give a tenth of all I get.'

But the tax collector stood at a distance. He would not even look up to heaven, but beat his breast and said, 'God, have mercy on me, a sinner.'

I tell you that this man, rather than the other, went home justified before God. For all those who exalt themselves will be humbled, and those who humble themselves will be exalted." (Luke 18:10–14)

Confidence and humility are the right combination. Your athletes are watching—how will you show and grow it for the team culture you're trying to build?

Do you let your players showboat because they can? Or do you win in a way that leaves the opponent with dignity?

Do you trash talk the player that left through the portal? Or do you wish him good luck and look forward to seeing how the rest of your team will have the chance to step up? How you choose to respond and move forward will set the tone for your team.

Character development is something that should be worked on every day. Be intentional. Develop strong habits that benefit those closest to you. As you lead by example and train your players, you are not only strengthening your team, but you are also helping your school, impacting your community, and building leaders. After all, your players today are tomorrow's husbands, fathers, employees, citizens, stars, and politicians.

> *Do not conform to the pattern of this world, but be transformed by the renewing of your mind. Then you will be able to test and approve what God's will is—His good, pleasing and perfect will.*
> *—Romans 12:2*

PART 4:
HOME PLATE

Make It Home

- 12 -

Carrying the Weight

*It's not the load that breaks you
down, it's the way you carry it.*
—Lou Holtz

WHETHER YOU ARE coaching for a Major League pennant contender or volunteering at the local high school, I don't know a single coach who doesn't feel like they're carrying more bricks than they can hold. Everyone has an expectation—managers, athletic directors, players, parents, spouses, bosses, maybe even sponsors or donors. Everyone needs a piece of you, and you only have so much time to give; there's only so much you can control. On the field or off, leaders carry the weight.

> ON THE FIELD OR OFF, LEADERS CARRY THE WEIGHT.

The summer of '68, I was invited to play American Legion Baseball in Bowling Green, Kentucky. As a 16-year-old with big dreams, I was excited to play with the best players from a five or six county area. I guess you could say it was our version of today's elite travel teams.

My parents supported me, but it was a sacrifice for me to drive me the 30 miles each way to practice three or four times per week. In order to help pay for the gas and food, I took a summer job at a feed mill nearby.

I'd often work all day, handling 50-pound feed sacks for $1.25 an hour. Then I'd drive into the city, pitch a nine-inning game, and then make the 30-mile drive back home.

My first week on the job, I was assigned the task of unloading the 50-pound sacks of feed from a train car and transferring them to the mill floor. I'd load them on a dolly five at a time, then attempt to guide them down a 15-foot steep ramp. I'd never used a hand-truck before. Every run, I'd lose control of the heavily weighted dolly as it sped down the ramp. The grizzled, career mill workers roared with laughter, calling me every unflattering synonym of stupidity as the dolly and 250 pounds of feed sacks sailed uncontrollably, dropping with a thud onto the floor.

After five or six difficult trips, someone in the group of full-time mill workers finally suggested I try taking the dolly down backwards—it worked! Although I still felt embarrassed by the names I'd been called, I was relieved not to have to pick up the sacks at the bottom of the ramp.

Any of the experienced men could have taken a minute to teach me how to make it down the ramp. Instead, they enjoyed the entertainment of watching me learn. The truth is, I probably wouldn't have listened. Like the average teenager, I'd have wanted to prove I could handle it on my own. Sometimes we aren't willing to listen until we've struggled.

During my 28 years of coaching, I didn't carry 250 pounds of feed on a dolly, but I carried the weight of my program. From recruiting and lineups, managing dugouts and staff, and holding players accountable for eligibility, to the win-loss record and expectations from administration, it sometimes it felt like the weight of the world.

I didn't always carry it well. Sometimes, I'd bring a loss or bad practice home with me. My family didn't deserve the task of helping me pick up the overweight sacks of stress. Carrying the weight for such a long time certainly didn't help me, my coaching staff, or my players.

One day, after a particularly bad practice, God showed me I needed to stop bringing the load home. It was the middle of the season, so my wife, Sharon, and my boys saw little of me between road trips and recruiting.

I should have had plenty of time to unwind and improve my attitude. Unfortunately, I spent the entire 25-minute drive home replaying all the mistakes my team had made. I wasn't in the mood to talk to anyone—selfishly, I just wanted to be alone. I thought it might be better for my family if I could spend a little time alone and away from them until dinner. I tend to be very quiet when I'm unhappy, which means that I wasn't a very good father or husband after any loss or bad practice. I pulled my vehicle into to the garage and opened the kitchen door, hoping to slip away.

As soon as the door opened, my youngest son, Tyler (10 years old at the time) wearing nothing but his gym shorts, socks, and a huge smile came sliding across the kitchen floor singing, "Dad, look at me! I'm a chubby boy!" It completely shook me out of my negative mood and gave us a good laugh together.

What on earth did I have to be down about? My family loved me whether we practiced poorly, or not. Suddenly, God helped me to realize just how very blessed I was. I determined that my family deserved a better version of me, and I was blessed to have them there for me on good and bad days.

Life's pressures can be challenging at times. If we take time to count our blessings, God often reminds us that there's more to life than winning or work.

All too often, leaders sacrifice the wrong things to reach goals and find success. It doesn't have to be that way. It shouldn't be that way. If your vision is big, bold, meaningful, and benefits others as well as your career, the appropriate sacrifices will be well worth it.

Put Your Priorities in Order

At the end of the day, at the end of your life, trophies won't matter if you've lost the people you want to celebrate the wins with. I'm certainly not perfect, but God graciously continues to remind me to keep my priorities in order. When I do, there's much deeper satisfaction in my life. And, not surprisingly, I bring a much better me to whatever I'm doing.

> AT THE END OF THE DAY, AT THE END OF YOUR LIFE, TROPHIES WON'T MATTER IF YOU'VE LOST THE PEOPLE YOU WANT TO CELEBRATE THE WINS WITH.

I've found priorities should be in this order:

1. *Family*
2. *Career/Work*
3. *Recreation and Relaxation*

Now, if you know me or you get my daily "Mound Visit" devotional texts, you may be saying, "Wait a minute, Keith. Where are God and faith in your list of priorities?"

I'm not leaving Him out, because we can all make God *number one* in each priority. Colossians 3:23 says, *"Whatever you do, work at it with all your heart, as working for the Lord, not for human masters."*

If we place God *first* in our family, our family life will be fulfilling and there will be less stress. We will honor

God by loving and serving our spouses, kids, siblings, and often aging parents.

If we place God *first* in our career, then it's not a job. It becomes part of our calling, and He will give wisdom and direction as we need it. Our career and our interaction with people will go much more smoothly. Our measure of success will likely have more to do with making an impact than making it to a certain level or achievement.

If we place God *first* in our recreation and relaxation time, we will enjoy it more. It's great to be thankful for time on the golf course, time on the lake, or time with family and friends hanging out by the grill or the firepit. We can thank God for these gifts, and it will give us more joy.

Take a Look at Your Stats

It's easy to tell ourselves we've got it. We're good. We know our priorities. But too often we don't stop and look at the numbers. If you had a stat sheet for how you spend the hours of your day, what would it really say?

How many waking hours did you spend with your family last week? If you are competing for husband of the year or father of the year honors, you may spend 20–30 waking hours with your family. That's an hour for dinner each evening and most of the weekend. If you're in-season or have teens in sports and activities, time spent with family is probably less.

What about hobbies, movies, or television? Yes, that includes watching ball games. Unless you're off-screen more than most and play golf, fish, or hunt, you likely spend 10–15 hours on recreation and relaxation.

How many hours did you spend with God last week? Let's assume that you are in the top 5% of all faithful people in our country and you spend an hour each morning in prayer and reading your Bible, plus you attend church for a couple of hours on Sunday. That means you are spending about 9 hours with God each week.

Don't forget your time at work. Include coaching and your day-job if they aren't the same. This could easily total 45–60 hours a week during the season.

DATE: _____ OPPONENT: _____

#	NAME	HOURS	CHANGE
1.	Work	45–60	
2.	Family	20	
3.	Rec. & Relaxation	15	
4.	God	9	
FLEX			
FLEX			

HEAD COACH: _____
ASST. COACHES: _____

According to my math, that means work comes in first (by a long shot), family second, recreation and relaxation third.

For those of you who say you place God first in your list of priorities, are you? By these stats, God comes in dead last.

I don't share this to cause guilt or shame. If any of us total the time we spend by what we say our priorities are, I bet none of us gets it right. Sometimes a simple look at our stats can show us our blind spots and help us make the adjustments we need so we're sacrificing the right things.

We all have the same 24-hour day. It's how we choose to use them that makes the difference.

As a leader, placing God first in your family, first in your career, and first in everything else you do will place yourself in a position to have success in every area of your life. There will be far more peace in your life. When we handle our tasks according to God's priorities, it's much easier to handle the load.

But seek first His kingdom and His righteousness, and all these things will be given to you as well.
—*Matthew 6:33*

- 13 -

Curve Balls

No one is useless in this world who lightens the burden of it to anyone else.
—*Charles Dickens*

BENDER, HAMMER, YELLOW hammer, Uncle Charlie, knee buckler...these are all terms baseball guys used to describe a curve ball. A pitch that's hard to handle. Sometimes we just have to face it, life throws curve balls. We can be checking all the boxes—living in our priorities, working hard, and making progress—when outside circumstances show up out of nowhere. Are you ready? The question isn't if curveballs come, it's a matter of how and when.

My curve ball came on a day that I will never forget. It was late summer, and I'd just pulled into the yard on my way home from practice. Sharon was mowing our property with our old Kubota tractor (one of my definitions of a good wife is one who will climb on a farm tractor and mow like a champion). It was a familiar scene on our property. But this particular day, I knew something was wrong.

Perhaps it was in her body language, or something I sensed in her spirit from 50 yards away. Either way, I knew. As I approached the tractor, she simply looked at me with sad, tear-filled eyes and said, "Keith, I may have cancer."

I'd just come off one of our best seasons ever at UK. Our boys were doing well in school and sports. The doctor hadn't thought the lump in her breast was anything to worry about, but Sharon knew. The biopsy proved her right.

The news shook our world. Sharon was only 39 years old. We had two boys, ages eight and ten. Suddenly, our lives were turned upside down.

The surgeon and oncologist told us that without chemo, she had a 50% chance of survival. I didn't like the math. However, with surgery, chemo, and a new drug, her chance improved to over 80%. Things moved quickly and she soon had a mastectomy followed by chemotherapy.

The fear of losing her and the realization that I wasn't in control created a whole new desire to be "present" anytime I was with her and our sons. Suddenly, every hour of every day was extremely important. I didn't want to waste a minute with negative moods because of losses and bad practices. I wanted each day with my family to count.

This was the heaviest burden that I had ever carried. My shoulders were heavy with the weight. Even though I was only 39, my chest felt tight with stress. I would catch Sharon staring off into space, knowing that she was, obviously, burdened to the max, as well. Within a few days after the surgery, we both were exhausted from restless nights, fear of the future, and feeling the weight of world on our shoulders.

One afternoon before the boys were home from school, we both thought a nap might help. We went into separate bedrooms hoping for rest—and not wanting to disturb the other if we tossed and turned.

It wasn't until after waking up that we discovered we'd both been praying as we lay in bed waiting for sleep to come. Our prayers were tearful and sincere. I told Sharon that it felt like Jesus was in the room with me saying, "Keith, if you let me, I will help you through this."

It wasn't audible, but it was one of the most profound spiritual experiences that I've ever had. I slept in peace and in confidence knowing God would help us in this journey. In an astonishing statement that helped my faith grow, Sharon said, "At that same time, the presence of Christ filled my room and told me the same thing!"

After this beautiful experience, Sharon clung to the Bible verse found in Colossians 3:15,

> *"Let the peace of Christ rule in your hearts, since as members of one body you were called to peace. And be thankful."*

The key words in this verse for both Sharon and me are *"let"* and *"be thankful."* Sometimes, in an odd quirk of human nature, we tend to cling tightly to our burdens. Instead, we need to let go—we need to give them to the One who is more than able to carry them. And be thankful!

> **SOMETIMES, IN AN ODD QUIRK OF HUMAN NATURE, WE TEND TO CLING TIGHTLY TO OUR BURDENS. INSTEAD, WE NEED TO LET GO—WE NEED TO GIVE THEM TO THE ONE WHO IS MORE THAN ABLE TO CARRY THEM.**

Sharon dealt with the diagnosis, surgery, and chemotherapy with grace and strength. Her faith was stronger than ever. We eventually had total peace with God about the brevity of life and what's important during the span of years that He gives to each one of us.

During these years with her battle with cancer, the baseball losses were left at the field where they belonged. I learned, for the most part, how to appreciate the precious present. It is a *gift*.

Thirty-four years later, after other surgeries and scares, our faith together continues to grow, and we are thankful for each day God gives us together.

Burdened for Others

Sometimes the burdens we hold in our hearts aren't for ourselves or our families. Sometimes we're weighed down with the hard knocks and the heartache of our players and colleagues.

The risk of getting to know your players is also knowing their struggles and sorrows. I've had players recovering from illness, breakups (yes, those are big), or their parents' divorce. I've had players wonder how they'll make it over the break. One player came to me recovering from the physical and emotional trauma of gun violence. Another nearly lost his eye in a wild accident on the field.

> **THE RISK OF GETTING TO KNOW YOUR PLAYERS IS ALSO KNOWING THEIR STRUGGLES AND SORROWS.**

The problems of life are quite cumbersome when you don't know how to carry them. The Apostle Peter said, *"Cast all your anxiety on him because he cares for you"* (1 Peter 5:7).

Guy Doud was a young language arts teacher in Minnesota who knew the struggles of leading and caring for the students in his classroom. Guy had an empathetic ear for the hurting students in his classroom. Some came to talk while others shared in class journals and assignments. Either way, he knew about their dysfunctional families. He listened to students as they would share with him about their parents' dependence on alcohol or drugs. He heard the cries of a young girl who confided in her journal that she'd been struggling and was even considering taking her own life.

The empathetic teacher began to reach out to the students who weren't popular and the ones who weren't that bright. He even sat with the athletes who never got a chance to play, even when games were won by a mile or never even in reach. He would hear the athletes say, "Mr. Doud, am I really that bad?"

The burden was heavy. Guy was on the brink of quitting and leaving for an "easier" career when he had a turning point.

One morning before any of the students arrived for his first period class, Guy was overwhelmed by all of his students struggles and heartaches. He happened to sit down in the desk of one of those students. As he sat there, he began to think about this particular first period student. Then, he began to pray for her. The next day, he sat in another desk and prayed for that student. Pretty soon he was sitting in a different desk daily and praying for the specific student who sat there.

A few years later, Guy Doud was honored with the National Teacher of the Year award. He is convinced, and so am I, that through prayer, God began allowing him to see his students in the way God sees them. "I sit down in Sean's desk, and I pray for Sean, sitting in his desk. And then, when Sean comes walking down the hall, I can never think of him again in the same way," I heard Guy share on a radio program.

Prayer is indeed a powerful tool for all of us. Whether we teach, coach, own a business, manage a team, or parent a child, prayer can change us and those we lead for the better.

Help with the Load

We don't have to be a Mother Teresa or a Billy Graham to pray. We don't have to be what many would call pious or good. We only need to talk to God and let him know what is on our hearts and what is troubling our minds. He can give us peace, rest, empathy for others, and wisdom and strength to help us as we lead. When I start my day asking Christ to help me with the load, the day goes much smoother.

After hearing Guy Doud speak, I began praying for my players one-by-one. Sometimes, when no one was around, I would walk around our field and pray for the players in the position they each filled.

The prayers never helped me win a National Championship or to be named Coach of the Year, but they sure helped me see my players and coaches in a new way. They helped me lead with empathy. They opened my heart to God's wisdom. And they helped my relationships within the team, many of whom I'm still in touch with today.

Some of the weighty problems we have are small compared to others, but they are still burdens. It's hard to prioritize the important things in our life when our hearts are heavy. We can't move and be productive as a coach when we have all these different issues weighing us down. God willingly takes them from us when we let go of them, giving us freedom of movement and thought. When I ask, Jesus doesn't only carry my load—He carries me as well.

> *Do not be anxious about anything, but in every situation, by prayer and petition, with thanksgiving, present your request to God. And the peace of God, which transcends all understanding, will guard your hearts and minds in Christ Jesus.*
> *—Philippians 4:6–7*

- 14 -

Heading for Home

*It's easy to make a buck. It's a lot
tougher to make a difference.*
—*Tom Brokaw*

I WAS AT A conference awhile back when Walt Wiley, my friend and former Atlanta Braves team chaplain, challenged the room full of baseball guys to define the importance of the lead-off man in the lineup.

"What's the number one goal of the lead-off hitter?" asked Wiley.

"To get on base," answered one coach.

"To see as many pitches as possible in order to share with the team what the pitcher's stuff is like and help get the pitch count up," said another.

A third astute baseball guy added, "To set the table for the power hitters in the lineup."

After a handful of good suggestions, Walt quietly and wisely gave the final answer: "The job of every lead-off hitter is to make it home."

Whether it's on the field or in life, it's isn't good enough in life to just "make it." Sure, it's nice when we can help the next guy or take a few pitches for the team. But ultimately, we need to learn how to make it to home plate—the finish line of a good life. With God's help, we can impact others, persevere through the challenges, and finish strong, impacting the game today as well as tomorrow's future.

Most players you coach will not play at the next level. Yet, they will all have the opportunity to become great people. One day they'll be employees, business owners, teachers, doctors, or nurses. They'll build someone's house or repair their car. They'll be a neighbor, a friend, and a family member.

> **MOST PLAYERS YOU COACH WILL NOT PLAY AT THE NEXT LEVEL. YET, THEY WILL ALL HAVE THE OPPORTUNITY TO BECOME GREAT PEOPLE.**

If you put all the emphasis on winning, you're going to come up short. There's always a better record, bigger trophy, or higher level to coach or play. The attitudes, issues, and pressures you face only grow.

However, if your focus is on building people, not only will your impact last, but the struggle will be worth it. The wins are so much bigger than the game, series, or season at hand.

Leaving a Legacy

We all have an opportunity to leave a legacy for those in our circle of influence. I'm not talking about fame or fortune. I'm talking about leaving people with something that helps them not only be a better player, but to live into their potential.

For most of the year, I meet weekly with a group of coaches and scouts to study the Bible and encourage each other. Recently, one of them shared this quote by Peter Strople: "Legacy is not leaving something for people. It's leaving something in people."

Jesus said it this way, *"But store up for yourselves treasures in heaven, where moths and vermin do not destroy, and where thieves do not break in and steal. For where your treasure is, there your heart will be also"* (Matthew 6:20-21).

What we leave "in" people is so much more meaningful than what we leave "for" people. When you know your own identity, build a vision, and create a winning culture, the legacy will be the outflow. It might be one small moment that makes the difference for a lifetime in an athlete.

Start the Right Ripple

During my playing career, most of my coaches made a positive impact, but there were a few whose negativity wore me down and temporarily robbed me of my joy and love for sports. When I look back at playing for them,

I see a young man with no joy hanging his head and feeling no hope. I spent an entire year with one coach and never heard a positive statement from him. I can still remember that season. On the other hand, all it takes is one moment, one statement of belief, to put a player on a positive trajectory.

That key moment came as a minor league player in the Montreal Expos organization. I signed with them as a free agent in the summer of '69, right out of high school. Since I was only 17 and it was already late June, the Expos and my parents decided it would be best for me to wait and start in the Gulf Coast League the following summer.

After my first year in college, I traveled down to Florida to train. I spent a short while at the spring training complex in West Palm Beach before being sent up the coast to Bradenton to play the Gulf Coast Rookie League. We stayed at Pirate City, the Pittsburg Pirates spring training facility. At the time, it was a fairly new complex located out of town with orange groves all around. We had players from four different organizations staying in the dorms near the fields.

My roommate, I'll call him Bobby, was a college grad from Chicago. He was a city guy with college under his belt. The Expos placed him with me—an 18-year-old country boy who was green as a gourd.

The routine at Pirate City was the same every day: wake up at 7:00 a.m., breakfast with all the players, into uniforms and on the field for practice from 9–11:30 a.m., lunch outside the locker room—hot soup with an apple and Tang (this was the drink of the first astronauts, after all), then an afternoon game against one of the other teams in the peak of the 90-degree Florida sun.

After the game we cleaned up and went back to the dorm to sit and stare at the walls until dinner. After dinner, it was back to the room with the same roommate and stare at the same walls. No television, no radio, no phones. We were basically stuck in the orange grove counting the days until we'd take a trip down to Sarasota to play under the lights in a real stadium (even if it was Minor League).

I was fine with the routine, but the college guys and the city boys were getting antsy, including my roommate. One night Bobby had had enough, "I'm going crazy. I feel like I'm in prison." He looked at me and said, "I'm calling a cab and going into town."

Whether it was kindness or feeling sorry for me, I'm not sure which, but he asked if I was coming along. I thought he was one of the coolest guys, so I jumped at the chance.

The cab picked us up—I had never ridden in a taxicab before—and headed toward Bradenton and then dropped us off at Publix. I remember thinking, *What are we doing spending money on a cab so we can hang out at the grocery store?* But I followed my leader. Before I knew it, Bobbly was talking to a cute girl at one of the checkout counters.

The young woman was engaged but she called her friends and eventually we found ourselves watching the sun set over the Gulf of Mexico. I started getting nervous about curfew. Bobby told us to leave, he and his friend would catch up later.

Back in my room at Pirate City, I began to worry about Bobby as the clock ticked closer and closer to our 11 o'clock curfew. At 11:15 p.m. there was a knock on the door. It was not Bobby ... instead, I opened the door to find our field manager, a former Major Leaguer and a baseball lifer who was tougher than nails.

"Where's your roommate?" he asked bluntly.

"Bobby's using the pay phone. He should be back any minute," I lied.

The coach went on his way, and I breathed a sigh of relief, hoping Bobby would show up soon. He didn't, but our manager did.

"Madison, you lied to me," the manager said. "And your roomie has some explaining to do. Both of you be in the office at 8:00 a.m. tomorrow morning."

When Bobby finally came in an hour later, I told him about the room check. He was sure I was joking.

"You're pulling my leg," he said.

"Nope." Then he finally believed me.

The next morning both Bobby and I were quiet as we sauntered over to the coach's office instead of breakfast.

Bobby was called in first. Just 15 minutes later he walked back into the waiting area. "That's it," he said. "Five games into my professional career and it's over. They released me."

Fear suddenly swept over me. In my mind, I'd made an even bigger mistake. I lied to the manager to cover for Bobby. My mind raced at how I would explain this to my parents. Just tell the truth, I guessed. I was already spinning on what I would say to my friends when Larry Doby opened the door and called, "Madison, come on in."

In case you missed that era of baseball history, Larry Doby had been a powerful slugger for the Cleveland Indians, Chicago White Sox, and Detroit Tigers. All of this came after his successful career in the Negro League and a stint in the Navy during World War II. Doby is best known as the second African American to play Major League Baseball, signed just three months behind Jackie Robinson. He was the first African American to play in the American League. Doby went through the same racist hell as Robinson, without as many accolades for having done it. He was a great player. As a coach, he had a commanding presence.

The second I stepped into the office our manager began unloading on me about lying to him about Bobby being on the phone. He was pointing his fingers in my face, saying things like, "We won't tolerate liars in our organization!" and, "What you did last night was a disgrace to the Expos organization." After having just watched Bobby leave for good, I knew my career was about to be over.

I remember tears welling up in my eyes as I experienced my dream ending so suddenly. That's when I felt a strong hand on my shoulder—it was Larry Doby's hand.

"Skipper, I see things differently," Doby said to the manager. "Yes, Madison lied, but he was protecting his teammate. If I were still playing, I would want a teammate like Madison, here, who would be willing to cover my butt if I messed up."

I was holding my breath waiting for what would come next. After what seemed like minutes, our manager said, "Madison, go put your uniform on and get ready to practice. But hear me well. Don't you ever lie to me again."

The weight of the world had been lifted off me. I could have been sent home that day, and there's a good chance my life would have taken a different path. But Larry Doby extended grace to me. He saw something more in my potential and went to bat for me to get a second chance.

I realize now that there was probably more to the story. Major League Baseball is a business, and age matters when scouts and coaches evaluate players. Bobby was 23. That was old for someone in Rookie League at that time. Management looks for reasons to eliminate the average player unless they are a prospect or a bonus baby. Every year players are moved up while others are moved out. I'm sure my age played a factor in the manager's willingness to give me another shot. Either way, that one moment changed the trajectory of my life and career.

The impact Larry Doby had on me has been with me since the summer of 1970. The grace and compassion he extended to me influenced the way I coached for all those years. When a coach uses his influence in a positive way, he can not only influence the young player in front of him, but also everyone that player touches in the future. One simple act of believing in someone can start the right ripple.

Be Patient

> ONE SIMPLE ACT OF BELIEVING IN SOMEONE CAN START THE RIGHT RIPPLE.

Be patient. It takes time to make an impact. We live in a day and age when everything is available at our fingertips. You can even have your fast-food meal delivered to your front door. Good things, deep things—like trust, rapport, and character—take time.

I know it doesn't seem like you have the luxury to wait to see results; not with the college transfer portal or even recruiting of younger players for competitive high school or travel ball teams. You're AD or parents may be asking for you to turn your program around yesterday. Don't give up on the process.

Remember, failure is not fatal. It's not a question of *if* injuries, bad calls, discouragement, losses, and internal problems will happen, it's *when* they will happen.

Setbacks are a part of life. It's having perseverance that gets us to the other side.

Who is Leading You?

I don't know any successful coach or leader who will honestly say they've done it all on their own. Just listen to an acceptance speech after a hall of fame induction or championship win. Every winner has a list of supporters: coaches, management, encouraging family and friends. I believe we all need something bigger than the game... faith.

Jesus Christ is the ultimate leader—He came from heaven to live and breathe and show us exactly what it looks like to help others. He hung out with fishermen, tax collectors, church guys, and businessmen. I think if He were on earth today, He'd hang out at a baseball field too.

He didn't just come to be with us—Jesus came to be the ultimate sacrifice, to give up His life by dying on a cross in our place. All we have to do is be willing to trust and follow Him. What better gift could we receive?

We all make mistakes. I know I'm not perfect—there is no perfect coach, perfect player, or perfect person. Jesus led a perfect life and showed us how to live life better. But He didn't stop at simply setting the standard. Jesus took every mistake, every failure, every hurt we've caused and paid the price for us. He chose to suffer and die on the cross to be the perfect sacrifice for our sins.

My favorite verse in the Bible was written by Paul, a man who persecuted Christians prior to meeting Christ on the road to Damascus. Once Paul met Jesus, his life changed dramatically and eternally. Listen to the words he wrote to the church in Corinth to explain who Jesus is: *"God made Him who had no sin to be sin for us, so that in Him we might become the righteousness of God"* (2 Corinthians 5:21).

As I was reading this verse one morning, God allowed me to understand it in a powerful way. I could see that while Jesus was on the cross, He was saying, "Keith, give them to me, I will take all your sins, past, present, and future and they will die on the cross with me. Then, He said, "Here, Keith, you can have my righteousness." I was able to understand that no one is good or righteous apart from Jesus. It's the Great Exchange; we give our sins to Jesus and, in return, He gives us His righteousness.

Following Jesus in our everyday lives doesn't have to be complicated. He promised to be with us wherever we are—even in the dugout. During the last two thirds of my coaching career, I would pause during the National Anthem to thank God for the brave men and women who fought for the freedoms we have and to ask Him to give wisdom to me as I made decisions during the game. I would ask God to help me have patience with my players and even the umpires. Most of the time, umpires needed patience with me!

The promise Jesus gives is that we are never alone. Yes, you need mentors and supporters. You can always use a strong group of fellow coaches to be encouragers and bounce ideas off of. But if you follow Jesus, you will never be alone. His wisdom, strength, and support are available at all times.

Find the Right Place

If you coach for any length of time (even two seasons), you're going to have to make choices on which program to work with. If you are always looking at the next job, the higher salary, the bigger program, it will be much harder to connect with players and have a lasting impact. Sometimes you'll need to stay, and other times the right move will be to go.

It's unusual to spend 25 years at one school like I did at UK. In fact, very few coaches spend their whole career in the same place. Often, a coach must do what is best for his family. That's why I left Lake Wales High School in my mid-20s.

When I started my career as a coach, I didn't have the dream of one day coaching at a Division 1 college program. I just wanted to coach baseball. After spending two years coaching at Lake Wales, I realized that coaching was more than just teaching young men how to better play the game. I loved Lake Wales and especially the players who played for me there. They inspired me and let me know that I was in the right profession for me. I trust and pray that I made an impact on them. I know they made an impact on me.

Making the decision to move to Mississippi State was not easy. At the time, we had no children, and I knew that I needed to further my education. I also knew leaving a full-time job would mean sacrifice.

Truth be told, I would have been content to teach and coach at the high school level for a long time ... perhaps for my entire coaching career. But people I trusted and who influenced me strongly encouraged me to attend graduate school and learn from one of the best coaches in baseball. The option was left open for me to return to Lake Wales and continue there. It turns out, my path led elsewhere.

Moving to Starkville marked a pivotal point in my career. The graduate assistantship opened doors for me that I never dreamed of entering. When I noticed the impact Head Coach Ron Polk had on his players and the entire baseball community, it opened my eyes for future opportunities. It eventually led me back to my home state of Kentucky and the opportunity to coach for the Wildcats.

It wouldn't be the last time I had to choose the right path. About twelve or thirteen years into my tenure at UK, I was offered an opportunity to coach at an even bigger school with better facilities, warmer weather, and in a fertile area for recruiting. My AD talked to me about the position and said with all honesty, "We can't do for you here what they can. We are years away from those facilities and that salary." I discussed the opportunity with my family and prayed, asking for God's wisdom. And then I told my AD that I wanted to stay at Kentucky. He was shocked.

Looking back on that decision, there are no regrets. The influence and the platform that God has given me in Kentucky is both humbling and rewarding. It wasn't about the money or facilities. It was about where I sensed God wanted me to coach and provide for my family. It was the field of influence He'd given me.

I understand the allure of competing at a higher level. The salary, the prestige, and the opportunity to coach better athletes is always appealing. Grow where you are planted first, and make sure that you continue to coach for the right reasons. If you do consider a move to another program, make sure it's a move that is best for your family and for what God has called you to do.

> GROW WHERE YOU ARE PLANTED FIRST, AND MAKE SURE THAT YOU CONTINUE TO COACH FOR THE RIGHT REASONS.

When I read the powerful and encouraging word that God spoke to Jeremiah, it is certain that He was also speaking to you and me, *"For I know the plans I have for you, declares the Lord, plans to prosper you and not to harm you, plans to give you hope and a future"* (Jeremiah 29:11).

God can give us that hope, that future. It may not be easy. There's no guarantee we won't face challenges or setbacks. But He can prosper in us and give us influence and a platform if our hearts and minds are open.

That future can be at the high school level or in travel ball, at the college level, or even in professional baseball in the US or abroad. No matter where you coach, you have a tremendous platform to pour into the lives of young baseball players. The passion for coaching and leading is from God, but He wants us to use that gift to influence people in a way that pleases and honors Him. He wants us to make that special connection with young people that will also help them prosper, have hope, and a future.

More Than the Average

The opportunities you have to be a positive influence in the life of young players is tremendous. Billy Graham, the famous preacher, once said, "A coach will impact more people in one year than the average person will in an entire lifetime."

People often assume Graham was talking about making a positive influence, and perhaps he was. In reality, our impact can be positive or negative. Your athletes will either remember you as the coach who helped them grow or the guy they never want to see again. You are making an impact either way. The real question is what kind of impact do you want it to be? That answer is entirely in your hands.

What an incredible honor it is to be called *Coach*. Yes, coaching is more than winning and losing ball games and running an efficient practice. It's also a journey that you take with young men through life. One former player performed surgery on my knee. I've heard several preach some strong sermons. I've watched dozens coach at various levels, and one manage a Major League team for years. I've seen many compete in front of thousands in MLB stadiums. Others have become successful businessmen, attorneys, physicians, farmers, and educators. I've picked one former player up at a homeless shelter. I've talked to two on their death beds, just minutes before they entered eternity. If we allow it to happen, we become a part of them, and they certainly become a part of us.

Baseball is a gift. Let's stay in the game and use our passion and skills to be champion level coaches who build championship people.

For we are God's handiwork, created in Christ Jesus to do good works, which God prepared in advance for use to do.
—Ephesians 2:10

Acknowledgments

GOD CREATES EACH one of us with certain gifts and personality traits, but He allows us to be influenced, taught, trained, and loved by people who help shape us into the person He wants us to be. He has blessed me with family, friends, teammates, coaches, and players who have each contributed to my life in abundant ways.

There is a well-known verse in the Gospel of John that describes profoundly who each of us can and can't be, depending on our relationship with Christ. *"I am the vine; you are the branches. If you remain in me and I in you, you will bear much fruit; apart from me you can do nothing"* (John 15:5). One thing I know, without Him this book would be just one man's ideas on how to coach and lead. Without Him it would be nothing. With Him, it can encourage and even enlighten people on how they can use their gifts to influence others in a positive way.

Writing this book was fun, challenging, frustrating, and overwhelming at times. There are a few people who encouraged me, spoke truth to me, and helped me when the going got tough. I would like to thank and acknowledge each one who helped me along this journey.

Tara Cooper was introduced to me through a friend, Katie Filiatreau. Katie had recently written *The Healing Path* with Tara's help. Tara became my "coach" for over a year. The stories, concepts, and thoughts are all mine, but Tara was the one with the game plan and the execution of the X's and O's of the book. She has coached, organized, edited, and motivated me along the journey. When I would reach a certain goal, she shared my excitement. And, when the process was confusing, she taught and gave direction like a championship coach. Like most excellent coaches, she started as a coach and finished as my friend. Thanks, Tara!

Kim Small at Xulon Press has been incredibly professional as she helped get my book into the hands of readers. Her patience and attention to detail have been an asset and a blessing.

It helps when your wife is an English teacher. It also helps when she believes in you. Sharon probably knows the content of this book as well as me. She was a part of my coaching and leadership journey, and she was certainly a wonderful sounding board and editor. She has the uncanny ability to know when I need her help and, also, when I need space to write, vent, or pray. Her attention to detail and her patience were much needed. Her unconditional love is a Godsend.

It also helps when one of your sons majored in English and is blessed with creativity and wisdom. Tyler lives twenty miles from us, so he made numerous trips to "pull me out of the ditch" and help make this project a reality. He designed the cover, edited, and added a few cool graphics. He also improved my website and encouraged me in his own quiet way.

Even though he lives 150 miles away, my oldest son, Austin, also encouraged me. It has been an education to witness his positive leadership and relationship skills. His example of getting back up after having been knocked down is an inspiration to me. He is my all-time favorite former player.

My mother, Geraldine, is 96 years young and continues to love and encourage her children. Like my father, she grew up during the Great Depression and World War ll. I'm still fascinated by her memories of childhood, her resourcefulness, and her strength. One of my earliest memories is listening through a slightly open bedroom door to her prayers for her children. She exemplifies the adage that some things are better caught than taught. I "caught" devotion to God and family from her. She is a treasure.

My father, Holman, is deceased, but his remarkable example of always giving your best effort and his strength of character was a godly example of excellence and the American Dream. During the Great Depression he was forced to drop out of high school to work on the family farm but overcame his tough childhood to become a great father and a wonderful provider. He never allowed me to drown in self-pity or blame someone else when

I failed. He taught me how to compete on the field and in life.

Thanks to each coach or manager I ever had. At some point, I figured out that each coach was for me, not against me. I learned to ignore the language and the negativity from a few and pick up on the point they were trying to make. To the coaches who poured positivity and taught skills with enthusiasm, God bless you, because I tried my best to emulate you. I must put in print those baseball coaches and managers who inspired me ... David Webb, KayDon Vanmeter, Charles Alexander, Mike Cobb, Jack Lamabe, Bob Oldis, Jimmy Bragan, and Russ Nixon. Without them, this book would have never made it to the "idea stage." There were many contemporaries who taught and mentored me, as well ... Joe Mangascle, Ron Polk, Mark Johnson, Jerry Kindall, Bob Bennett, Dave Keilitz, and Hal Baird. Some have gone on before me and others still motivate and teach me.

There are many who encouraged me to put some of my coaching philosophy and experiences on paper. I will always be grateful to Adam Hunt, Lee Webb, John Huang, and Katie Filiatreau for saying, "Just do it!"

There are also those who prayed for the writing of this book. My four Dixie Café guys, John Swaim, Royce Bourne, Larry Winkleman, and Dale Hale, all committed early on to pray for this project.

Finally, Tom and Phil Arington. This father-son duo has supported my efforts in a phenomenal way. It's humbling to have friends who believe in you and who support you. I am thankful in a heartfelt, sincere way.

All the people mentioned have been great teammates. My prayer is that they will know my gratitude and that God will be glorified in the pages of *Coaching with Purpose.*

Notes

Chapter 1
Hans Urs von Balthasar, "What you are is God's gift to you...": Goodreads, accessed June 2024. https://www.goodreads.com/work/quotes/254351-das-betrachtende-gebet

Craft a vision, build alignment, champion execution: Using the three fundamentals of leadership defined in *The Work of Leaders* as inspiration, we'll look at how they play out for baseball coaches. Straw, Julie, Barry Davis, Mark Scullard, and Susie Kukkonen. *The Work of Leaders*. Pfeiffer & Company, 2013.

Chapter 2
"You see, you spend a good piece of your life gripping baseball...": Jim Bouton. Goodreads, accessed December 2023. https://www.goodreads.com/quotes/330429-you-see-you-spend-a-good-piece-of-your-life

"We leave something of ourselves behind...": Pascal Mercier. "Night Train to Lisbon Quotes." *Quotes.net*. STANDS4 LLC, 2024. Web. 31 Oct. 2024. https://www.quotes.net/mquote/1045895

Chapter 3

"A vision is not just a picture of what could be…": Rosabeth Moss Kanter as quoted by Daly, John. "A Vision is Not Just a Picture of What Could Be; It's Really So Much More!" Coach to Expect Success, April 4, 2015. (accessed March 2024) https://www.coachtoexpectsuccess.com/coach-dalys-blog/a-vision-is-not-just-a-picture-of-what-could-be-its-really-so-much-more

"If you don't know where you're going…": Yogi Berra. "Yogi-isms," Yogi Berra Museum & Learning Center, accessed March 2024, https://yogiberramuseum.org/about-yogi/yogisms/

"There are three types of baseball players…": Tommy Lasorda. Brainy Quote, accessed April 2024. https://www.brainyquote.com/quotes/tommy_lasorda_139458

"Character—or lack of it—is…": Ken Blanchard. Blanchard, Ken and Mark Miller, *The Secret: What Great Leaders Know and Do*, Berrett-Kohler, revised and updated 2014.

Chapter 4

"Before I can live with other folks…": Harper Lee in *To Kill a Mockingbird*. Goodreads, "Harper Lee Quotes," accessed March 2024. https://www.goodreads.com/quotes/9157-they-re-certainly-entitled-to-think-that-and-they-re-entitled-to

Henri Nouwen's Five Lies of Identity: Frank, Tobe. "Lies and Truth of Identity," *Tobe Frank: Thinking Honestly about Life and Faith,* July 9, 2019. https://www.tobefrank.com.au/i-like-this-quote/lies-and-truth-of-identity/

Chapter 5

"People buy into the leader...": John Maxwell. Maxwell, John. *21 Irrefutable Laws of Leadership,* Thomas Nelson, 1998.

Simon Sinek on a why and a vision: "Is a WHY or a vision more important?" by Simon Sinek, YouTube, April 13, 2020, https://youtu.be/olX3quSd4Eg?si=MEMVvTnRMCQpN0zz

Chapter 6

"Leaders have three fundamental responsibilities...": Straw, Julie, Barry Davis, Mark Scullard, and Susie Kukkonen. *The Work of Leaders*. Pfeiffer & Company, 2013.

"Listening is an art...": Dean Jackson. "In the Age of Noise, Are We Listening Enough?" *The Daily Coach*, Substack, March 6, 2020. https://thedailycoach.substack.com/p/listening-in-an-age-of-distraction

"You can't hire and fire your children...": Simon Sinek on leading with empathy. "Most Leaders Don't Even Know the Game They're In," Simon Sinek keynote from Live2Lead with John Maxwell, Atlanta, GA, October

7, 2016. YouTube, November 2, 2016. https://youtu.be/RyTQ5-SQYTo?si=Fh88rk1iOmroEA4S

Chapter 7

"**The interesting thing about coaching is...**": Ric Charlesworth. "Quotes from Coaches to Keep You Motivated," *Gloveworx*, April 3, 2018. https://www.gloveworx.com/blog/quotes-coaches-keep-you-motivated/

"**Words are seeds...**": Anonymous poem. Economy, Peter. "26 Brilliant Quotes on the Super Power of Words," *Inc.com*, November 5, 2015. https://www.inc.com/peter-economy/26-brilliant-quotes-on-the-super-power-of-words.html

"**You can't think and hit at the same time.**": Yogi Berra. Neumann, Thomas. "Yogi Berra quotes: ESPN.com celebrates the wit, wisdom of a baseball legend," *ESPN.com*, September 23, 2015. https://www.espn.com/mlb/story/_/id/13722210/yogi-berra-quotes-celebrating-late-great-new-york-yankees-legend

"**The more attention you pay to a behavior...**": Ken Blanchard. Thomas, Damien. "Ken Blanchard Quotes About Leadership," *Your Positive Oasis*, August 34, 2021. https://yourpositiveoasis.com/25-ken-blanchard-quotes-about-leadership/

Chapter 8

"When team members connect...": Jon Gordon. "When team members connect and build trust and strong relationships they don't just work with each other, they work for each other." @jongordon11 on *X* (formerly Twitter), July 18, 2018. https://x.com/jongordon11/status/1019729075269718016

"There is no 'I' in team, but there is an 'I' in win.": Nick Saban. As heard in an interview and originally written in his book, *How Good Do You Want to Be?: A Champion's Tips on How to Lead and Succeed at Work and in Life.* Ballantine Books, 2004. Goodreads, accessed October 2024. https://www.goodreads.com/quotes/5275968-the-disease-of-me-dominance-lesson-1-there-is-no

"As Lily Tomlin once said...": Ken Blanchard. Quotefancy, accessed May 2024. https://quotefancy.com/kenneth-h-blanchard-quotes/page/3

Chapter 9

"Science is organized knowledge...": Immanuel Kant in *Critique of Practical Reason.* Goodreads, accessed February 2024. https://www.goodreads.com/quotes/11808796-science-is-organized-knowledge-wisdom-is-organized-life

Buck Showalter on analytics: "Baseball Stories: Episode 5 with Buck Showalter," *Baseball Stories*, interview by Jason

Stark, posted on May 1, 2018, YouTube, https://youtu.be/e2pTyAuUSEI?si=CCI05yOPVOYdsrFw

Terry Francona on analytics: "Terry Francona on Using Analytics," *Baseball Stories*, interview by Jason Stark, posted on May 1, 2018, YouTube, https://youtu.be/w9E1fOaIkBM?si=DVUr6z4oCmk9YIZB

"Wisdom is not a product of schooling...": Albert Einstein. Quotation, accessed March 2024. https://quotation.io/quote/wisdom-product-schooling-lifelong-attempt

"What would my successor do?": Craig Groeschel. "Secrets of Superior Decision Making," *The Craig Groeschel Leadership Podcast*, https://open.life.church/training/225-craig-groeschel-leadership-podcast-secrets-of-superior-decision-making

"If you can't stand the heat, get out of the kitchen.": Attributed to and popularized by President Harry Truman. Writing Explained, accessed April 2024. https://writingexplained.org/idiom-dictionary/cant-take-the-heat-get-out-of-the-kitchen

Chapter 10

"With everything that has happened to you...": Wayne Dyer. Mayberry, Matt. "Remembering Wayne Dyer: 20 Inspirational Quotes to Help You Become a Better You," *Entrepreneur*, July 19, 2016. https://www.entrepreneur.

com/leadership/remembering-wayne-dyer-20-inspirational-quotes-to-help-you/250142

Tye Cobb batting average: "Britannica, The Editors of Encyclopaedia. "Ty Cobb". *Encyclopedia Britannica*, 1 Oct. 2024, accessed November 1, 2024. https://www.britannica.com/biography/Ty-Cobb

"It's not about you.": Rick Warren. Warren, Rick. *The Purpose Driven Life*. Zondervan, First edition, October 8, 2002.

Chapter 11

"Character is doing the right thing...": J. C. Watts Jr. in *What Color is Conservative?: My Life and My Politics* https://www.goodreads.com/quotes/449975-character-is-doing-the-right-thing-when-nobody-s-looking-there

Percent of students who report cheating: "Cheat or Be Cheated? What We Know About Academic Integrity," Challenge Success, May 14, 2021. https://challengesuccess.org/resources/cheat-or-be-cheated-what-we-know-about-academic-integrity/

"Children are 25 percent of the population but 100 percent of the future...": Thomas Lickona. Lickona, Thomas. *Character Matters*. Atria Books, original edition, 2004.

Mikey Mantle: *Seattle Times* News Service. "Mickey Mantle: Remembering A Legend — Power To Transcend The Game — Greatness On The Field Indisputable," *Seattle Times,* August 14, 1995. https://archive.seattletimes.com/archive/19950814/2136474/mickey-mantle-remembering-a-legend——power-to-transcend-the-game——greatness-on-the-field-indisputable

Babe Ruth: "Babe Ruth," *Biography*, updated April 7, 2021. https://www.biography.com/athletes/babe-ruth

Pete Rose: Clark, Dave. "Why Pete Rose, aka Charlie Hustle, Sprinted to First Base After a Walk," *Cincinnati Enquirer* online, October 1, 2024. https://www.cincinnati.com/story/sports/mlb/reds/2024/10/01/pete-rose-charlie-hustle-nickname-sprint-first-base-walk-reds-hall-fame-mickey-mantle-enos-slaughter/75463380007/

Chapter 12

"It's not the load ...": Lou Holtz. What Should I Read Next, accessed April 2024. https://www.whatshouldireadnext.com/quotes/lou-holtz-it-s-not-the-load-that

Chapter 13

"No one is useless in this world...": Charles Dickens in *Our Mutual Friend*. Charles Dickens Info, accessed March 2024. https://www.charlesdickensinfo.com/quotes/no-one-is-useless-in/

Guy Doud story: "Teacher of the Year (Part 1 of 2)," *Focus on the Family with Jim Daly*, January 27, 2021 (original air date September 6, 1988). https://www.focusonthefamily.com/episodes/broadcast/teacher-of-the-year-part-1-of-2/

Chapter 14

"It's easy to make a buck. …": Tom Brokaw. "Tom Brokaw Quotes," AZquotes, accessed September 2024. https://www.azquotes.com/author/1946-Tom_Brokaw

"Legacy is not leaving something for people. …": Peter Strople. Editorial Team. "65 Insipiring Quotes about Leaving a Legacy," Saint Diamonds, August 12, 2024. https://www.saintdiamonds.com/blog/65-inspiring-quotes-about-leaving-a-legacy/

Larry Doby: Kernan, Kevin. "Larry Is the Stuff of Legends: Struggles for Doby a Lesson for Any Time," *New York Post*, July 28, 2002. https://nypost.com/2002/07/28/larry-is-stuff-of-legends-struggles-of-doby-a-lesson-for-any-time/

"Larry Doby," National Baseball Hall of Fame, https://baseballhall.org/hall-of-famers/doby-larry

"A coach will impact more people in one year…": Billy Graham. "Billy Graham Quote," AZquotes, accessed February 2024. https://www.azquotes.com/quote/825836#google_vignette

About the Author

KEITH MADISON IS a baseball lifer. He signed with the Montreal Expos at age 17 and was hired to lead the Kentucky Wildcat baseball program at 26. In his 28 years of coaching, he amassed over 800 wins. He has been inducted into five halls of fame, including the American Baseball Coaches Association (ABCA) Hall of Fame, the Kentucky Sports Hall of Fame, and the University of Kentucky Athletic Hall of Fame.

In 2013, the ABCA honored Madison with its most prestigious award, the Lefty Gomez Award, given for a lifetime of service in baseball both nationally and internationally. Madison has traveled to the Dominican Republic more than 30 times helping conduct free baseball clinics and share his faith with thousands of young Dominican baseball players and coaches.

Madison continues to support baseball coaches through his work with SCORE International and serving as a board member for the ABCA. You can find him in the radio booth doing color for Wildcats Baseball on the UK Sports Network or writing for *Inside Pitch* magazine. His most precious time is spent with his wife, Sharon, two grown sons, and cheering for his grandkids. He loves mentoring coaches, speaking, fishing, and keeping the lines straight with his zero-turn mower.

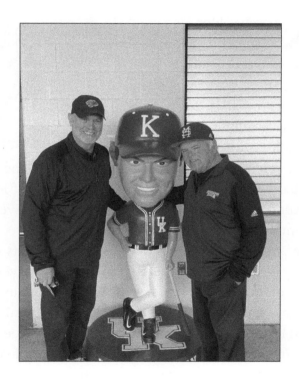

Coach Keith Madison and Coach Ron Polk

About the Author

Keith and Sharon Madison

MOUND VISITS
For more encouragement from Coach Madison, check out his daily Mound Visits. The short notes are a great way to start your day.

Go to coachkeithmadison.com

FOLLOW COACH KEITH
On *X* (Twitter) @keithmadison32
Instagram @keithmadison

Milton Keynes UK
Ingram Content Group UK Ltd.
UKHW040349111224
452348UK00001B/18